# The New Mas

## Finding your feet on the Square

Conceived, Written & Designed by

### Kim March PM

*I will strive with love & care*

*Upon the Level. By the Square*

Baal's Bridge Square inscription dated 1507

*Presented to*

By: ...........................................................

Occasion: ...................................................

Date: .........................................................

Lewis Masonic

First published 2020

ISBN 978 0 85318 574 1

Published by Lewis Masonic
an imprint of Ian Allan Publishing Ltd,
Shepperton, Middx TW17 8AS.
Printed in England.

Visit the Lewis Masonic website at
www.lewismasonic.co.uk

## Acknowledgements

I extend sincere thanks to everyone who has helped me to take *The New Mason's Friend* from a speculative outline concept to a published reality.

To expand my knowledge of medieval masonry and trade apprenticeships, I am particularly indebted to the authors of three books:

*Growing Up in Medieval London* Barbara A Hanawalt Oxford University Press 1993
ISBN 9780195093841

*The Medieval Mason* Douglas Knoop MA & *G. P. Jones* M. A. Professor of Economics and Lecturer in Economic History respectively, in the University of Sheffield. The Manchester University Press – 1933 – Out of Print – sourced through Abe Books rare books.

*The Time Traveller's Guide to Medieval England* Ian Mortimer. Vintage – 2009
ISBN 9781845950996

### Sincere Thanks to:

W Bro Dr **Richard Johnson**, a member of Brigantes Lodge No 9734 who reviewed my work from a historical perspective.

W Bro **Trevor McKeown** – Curator of the Vancouver Masonic Library and Archives – who kindly assisted me despite the Masonic library being temporarily warehoused awaiting its new home in 2021! Sincere, fraternal best wishes for the impending relocation.

All at **Lewis Masonic** for keeping Masonic publishing alive and kicking through the Covid-19 pandemic, including the publication of this book. I could not have done this without your invaluable support.

The **Salopian Lodge of Charity No 117** for allowing me to photograph their venerable collar jewels. **The Lodge (Masonic Regalia)** - www.thelodgeroom.co.uk for permission to publish their images of our present day collar jewels.

All the other photographers and illustrators who kindly making their artwork available under a free or commons creatives licence.

Last, but not least, my wife Sue, for all the tea and human spell check wizardry!

*Kim March*

## Other Image Credits

Every effort has been made to identify and attribute images – any errors are entirely unintentional.
**Front Cover:** Handshake (adapted) – Freeimages.com/ Henk L ● **Pixaby**: Windsor Castle image by *Falco* ● Medieval scissors by *kerttu* ● Hills Panorama by *Aalmeidah* ● Stone Chiseller & Stone Face (adapted) by *Tlintypephotos* **Shuttlestock.com images:** Peasant Boy by *Tntk* ● Henry IV statue by *Chris Dorney* ● Shrewsbury Old Market Hall by *D. Pimborough* ● Medieval Gothic Window by *MSSA* ● Medieval hammer by *Sergio Foto* ● Carved Head Gargoyle by *Electric Egg* ● Old Stone Carving Tools by *Sergio Foto* ● Forget me not flower by *Bo Valentino* ● All Seeing Eye by *Live Vector* ● London Bridge 1616 by *Morphart Creation* ● Silver Groat by *Sponner* ● Kings Solomon's Temple by 3*DMI* ● Bowline knots by *Jannarong* ● Wells Cathedral Scissor Arch by *Jacek Wojnarowski* ● Stone carver by *Sergio Foto* ● B&W medieval pavement by *PTDZ* ● Three Columns illustration by *Julie A. Felton* ● 3D Smooth/Rough Ashlar by *Marietjie* **Common Creatives Licensing:** Figure of King Athelstan by *alh!* ● (CC BY-ND 2.0) Fan Vaulting in King's College Chapel by *Philip Halling* (CC BY-SA 2.0) ● Pythagoras by *Naufragio* (CC BY-SA 2.0) Silhouettes of EAFM figures (3) all adapted from Creative Commons, unknown creator. licenced sources.

**Other Masonic Sources:** Lodge room viewed through Lewis courtesy Exmouth Masonic Hall, Devon – www.exmouthfreemasons.org ● Wardens Columns (adapted) courtesy www.pglrossandcromarty.org.uk ● Baal's Bridge Square courtesy of Vancouver Masonic Library and Archives, freemasonry.bcy.ca.

**Kim March:** Euclid's Proof illustration ● Phone keypad ● Progressive Offices ● Medieval Creeing Trough ● Berwick upon Tweed fortifications ● Masonic Memorial Garden (2) ● Grand Lodge Chart (excluding Creative Commons icons) ● Tau ● EAFM, FC & MM Aprons ● Grand Lodge Aprons ● MCF Booklet ● 'Mercury' collar jewel ● Ceremonial sword blade and hilt ● Lodge Layout Plans (2) ● Past Master's Collar jewel 1911 ● Chaplain's collar jewel ● Senior Steward's collar jewel ● Secretary's collar jewel ● Almoner's collar jewel ● Kings Solomon's Temple floor plan ● 5-MR logotype and illustrations ● Formation of Memory chart.

## Introduction..

*The New Mason's Friend* has been created to help new and inexperienced Brethren find their feet on the Square. So, let me introduce you to a friend who knows much of the information I wish I had in the very early stages of my own Masonic journey. A friend who shares their knowledge succinctly in everyday conversational English, set out in the six sections below:

## Six Part Contents Summary:                              Pages

In no time at all, you will have the best possible understanding of the perfect points of your entrance into Freemasonry!

Your new Masonic friend awaits you ...

***Kim March***

# Part 1

# 25 Questions about Freemasonry

$$a^2 + b^2 = c^2$$

# What is Freemasonry?

Ask an experienced Brother, 'What is Freemasonry?' and expect the answer:

### *A peculiar system of morality,*

### *veiled in allegory,*

### *and illustrated by symbols*

But what does that actually mean in present day language?

Let us break it down into its three component phrases:

## A peculiar system of morality …

The use of the word 'peculiar' in this context does not mean odd or unusual, but rather that of being distinctive, special or unique. The primary purpose of the system is to help us make morally founded self-improvements over our lifetime. So, let us settle on 'a unique system of self-improvement' – unique because there is no other comparable system.

## veiled in allegory …

An allegory is defined as a story, poem, or image that can be interpreted to reveal a hidden moral meaning. Freemasonry's stories are presented in three progressive Ceremonies; effectively three moral playlets. Each Ceremony is set in a different part of King Solomon's Temple for example, the principal part of the Ceremony of Initiation is set within the Temple's entrance or porchway. The allegorical messaging is consequently gradually revealed in three distinct stages. Let us run with 'gradually revealed in Masonic Ceremonies'.

## and illustrated by symbols

There are around 60 Masonic symbols, some of the best known are revealed and explained during the course of Craft Ceremonies – each a material object (or image thereof) to which an alternative, abstract meaning has been attached. Their function is to make us think in a broad, contemplative manner that can be simply summarised as 'moralising'. So, we might say 'working with objects given morally founded, alternative meanings'.

*A unique system of self-improvement*
*gradually revealed in Masonic Ceremonies*
*working with objects*
*given morally founded,*
*alternative meanings*

Through its philosophical teachings, 'speculative' Freemasonry is very much in the character building business, with the compounding effects of a large, global membership yielding enduring social benefits all around the world.

**Note:** Speculative Freemasonry is also referred to as 'The Craft' or 'Craft Freemasonry' because it was originally modelled the on the craft and ethical practices of medieval working Stone Masons, we refer to as being 'Operative Masons'. 'Operative Freemasonry' requires the skilful use of handheld tools; 'Speculative Freemasonry' requires the well considered application of our mental faculties.

**Note:** *The three Craft Degree Ceremonies are the:*

**First Degree**     **Ceremony** *of* **Initiation**     Rank:  **Entered Apprentice** [EA]

**Second Degree**  **Ceremony** *of* **Passing**     Rank:  **Fellow Craft** [FC]

**Third Degree**     **Ceremony** *of* **Raising**     Rank:  **Master Mason** [MM]

**Note:** *There is also an annual 'Ceremony of Installation' for installing the succeeding Worshipful Master for the ensuing 12 months*

# How does Freemasonry's Philosophy Work?

Freemasonry and the game of golf share a number of principles; contrasting these should improve our understanding of the former's philosophical virtues:

## 1]      Both are wholly dependent on faith

**Golfers:** Need to absolutely believe they can execute any intended shot – mindlessly 'hitting and hoping' arguably is not playing golf, but rather a futile application of time and energy. The need for faith is most apparent when playing a shot over a potentially intimidating hazard such as a body of water etc. There is an imperative need to believe, in order to achieve the intended shot, or else yet another golf ball will be consigned to a watery grave!

*Freemasons: Faith, in some physical or spiritual form, ultimately binds everything in our universe together. As Freemasons, we share a belief that each of us is accountable to a Supreme Being, with or without the need to subscribe to a particular religion. Early 20th century psychiatrists called this sense of connectivity to a higher authority 'Cosmic Consciousness', a phenomenon undoubtedly widely experienced by humankind since the dawn of time. The core moral codes of all the accepted religious beliefs are very similar, if not identical in many respects, e.g. forbidding murder, theft etc. It is therefore possible to collectively refer to such shared, common moral teachings as 'the Volume of the Sacred Law' (VSL). For Freemasons subscribing to a particular religious belief, the term 'VSL' serves as a euphemism for their religion's holy book. Faith is the cement that binds us as Freemasons together – each of us ultimately accountable to a higher authority for our words and actions.*

## 2]      Participants need to be honest with themselves

**Golfers:** Who blame anything for poor play, other than themselves, are not necessarily confronting reality. They are unlikely to improve their standard of play because they fail to acknowledge and analyse their mistakes in both temperamental (internal) and environmental (external) contexts. In effect, they are denying themselves the opportunity of making any meaningful improvements. Such attitudes doom any golfer to a lifetime of miserably foraging in the rough (or beyond) in the quest of the lost golf ball.

*Freemasons:* Recognise and accept that the dual journeys of self-discovery and self-improvement require a starting point of complete self-honesty. Improvements cannot be made without first perceiving and acknowledging imperfections of character, judgement, lack of knowledge and consideration of others etc. Whilst even some golf playing Freemasons may periodically search for lost balls, all Freemasons continuously inwardly search for the truth about themselves within the positive outward looking context of also benefitting the wider world. In some large part, this is what makes Freemasonry a truly personal journey – some philosophers might say that such intimate discoveries about their self are a Freemason's real secrets.

## 3] Both require patience, industry and perseverance

**Golfers:** The impatient player hits the course after a single lesson; they have neither read the rules of golf, nor studied the accepted etiquette. There is a huge imbalance between ability and expectation quickly giving rise to disappointment, frustration and possibly even anger. For the want of knowledge and tuition, any amount of practice is unlikely to result in a meaningful improvement of skills – repeated errors will, most likely, become more ingrained. In such frustrating circumstances, many aspiring golfers will ultimately give up the game for the want of pleasure, sense of achievement and satisfaction.

*Freemasons:* Recognise that being Initiated into the Craft does not bestow any instant Masonic benefits, but rather marks the beginning of a new learning based approach to life. The term 'progressive science' discloses that Freemasonry's teachings are gradually revealed to us over time calling for patience. We quest for self-improvement by way of taking one, well balanced, step at a time. We have our whole lifetime in which to practise and perfect every new lesson afforded by our journey of self-discovery.

*The parable of the Hare and the Tortoise springs to mind!*

## 4]    Both are products of the mind and body

**Golfers:** In golf the true opponent is the 'self' – no one else strikes the golf ball, but the player with the club physically planted in their hands with an envisaged shot clearly in mind. Consequently, to play the game very well requires a perfect balancing of both mind and body. In addition to staying physically fit, many professional golfers give considerable weight to the influences of the mind in their coaching programmes, often including 'positive thinking' and 'visualisation' strategies.

*Freemasons: The Masonic processes are all initiated in the cinema of the mind, ultimately translating into positive changes in outlook, views of the world and well judged actions. As these changes gradually evolve over time, they may initially seem to be barely discernible to us, but those closest to us will begin to see things somewhat differently. Ultimately, it is down to us as individuals to embrace Masonic teachings (mind) translating these into well considered, demonstrable actions (body).*

## 5]    Both are exposed to the uncontrollable influences of the wider world

**Golfers:** In planning their perfect play, golfers have to make allowances for hazards such as bodies of water, bunkers, overhanging trees etc and the effects of the prevailing weather. They are not in control of these and some, such as the wind, can be so variable from tee to green, that their effects are difficult to predict. Such factors provide an additional level of testing of both skill and judgement, which is why even some Masonic golfers occasionally find themselves searching in the rough.

*Freemasons: Freemasonry's teachings, symbols and secrets helps to build character, confidence, competence, and the wisdom of good judgement over our lifetime, preparing us to deal with the unpredictable gyrations of the wider world. We just need to get into the habit of routinely working with Freemasonry's teachings and consciousness tools. This can be facilitated by our regular attendance of Lodge and making a little time each day to further our Masonic knowledge. Practice always travels towards improvement and a better understanding and management of the ups and downs of everyday life.*

## 6] Sharing experiences raises knowledge and performance levels

**Golfers:** It is a long recognised golfing wisdom that playing with a more skilful opponent or partner raises the game of an inexperienced golfer. A combination of on course coaching, observation and heightened concentration yields powerful, performance enhancing benefits.

*Freemasons: Both Operative and Speculative Freemasonry have a long standing tradition of experienced Brethren transferring their knowledge to succeeding generations. Even Freemasonry's oldest document (Regius Poem c. 1425-1450) makes the point that maintaining silence to listen to a more experienced Brother best serves to raise a new Brother's level of understanding. This is very much the ethos of the Lodge of Instruction in Speculative Freemasonry. However, Craft Emulation Ritual first became widely available in printed form in 1969, enabling Brethren to learn Ritual independently at home. Previously, any unwritten Ritual was memorised in the medieval oral tradition of being verbally passed from Brother-to-Brother, from one generation to the next. It now seems that a renaissance of Lodges of Instruction is well underway, recognising the highly beneficial value of Brethren of all ages* 'sharing their experiences and knowledge'.

## 7] One vital difference!

**Golfers:** Many golfers consider the pinnacle of perfection to be the achievement of a hole in one. According to one source, the average golfer needs 12,000 complete rounds of golf to experience the delights of a single hole in one event. At least there is a slight chance of attaining golfing perfection!

*Freemasons: Despite recognising and accepting that absolute perfection is unattainable in our mortal lives, nevertheless, this does not deter us from endeavouring to make the best possible advancements in the joyous celebration of simply being human. To quote from a translation of a Masonic Lecture for Entered Apprentice Freemasons presented in Dresden on 16 December 1809.* '... it is the great and beautiful art to be human, to join sociably to fellow human beings, and then work together, so that humanity can reach its destiny on earth ever more complete and more beautiful.'

# How does Symbolism Work?

Take a look at the 'phone keypad layout opposite and have a go at answering this question - which four characters do you think are the oldest in origin?

If you picked either the asterisk or hashtag, you would be right – both these shapes feature in a database of European Ice Age cave art images, scientifically dated as ranging from 10,000 to 40,000 years old. You would also be OK if you picked the figures '1' or '0' as these shapes approximate to two other database constituents.

Paleoarchaeologist, Genevieve von Petzinger, examined 52 European Ice Age cave sites identifying 32 geometric shapes, regularly depicted on cave walls, painted by humankind over a 30,000 year term. The obvious question is, 'Did these shapes hold any symbolic meaning at the time of their creation?' If they did not, then why do they occur in so many sites over such a long period?

It seems most likely that some, if not all, of these 32 shapes functioned as symbols – each holding a shared meaning, now lost to us.

A symbol functions as a cerebral shortcut, prompting our recall of a complex concept that has previously been shown and explained to us. A single symbol can consequently communicate several paragraphs of text, but symbols should not be confused with icons. The home screens of our smart phone, laptop, desktop PC etc are loaded with icons, not symbols. Application icons simply remind us that the underlying programs are resident on our electronic devices whilst also functioning as 'tap to open' front doors.

During our Ceremony of Initiation, both the operative and symbolic significances of three working tools were explained to us – in Emulation Ritual this explanation comprised around 190 words, averaging a little over 60 words per symbol. So, symbols prompt the recall of concepts (complete stories) which icons do not.

Masonic symbols are gradually revealed and explained over a period of time. For this reason, Freemasonry is described as being a 'progressive science' – a phased process of enlightening teaching by way of symbolic revelations.

Symbolism is interpreted by the righthand side of the human brain – it operates in the abstract – the receiving brain interprets a meaning from the symbol, ideally as conceived and intended by the symbol's originator. Sometimes it evokes an emotional response as the receiver tries to envisage the originator's emotional state at the time of creating the symbol. This phenomenon also forms the basis of art appreciation. Imagine going into an Ice Age cave and seeing the outline of a real human hand painted 20,000 years ago. Someone sat down with their hand held firmly against the cave wall spitting homemade ferrous based paint which, once dried, enabled the artist to remove their hand. It would be very tempting to place the palm of our own hand over such an image – we would somehow feel more emotionally connected to the Ice Age artist – a 20,000 year old handshake!

Rather like advertising, symbolism also requires repetition to work at optimum efficiency. So, if we were told and accepted that the '#' sign symbolically represents, 'that our experience of Freemasonry is considerably enhanced by our making a daily advancement of Masonic knowledge', we would be reminded of this each time we saw a '#'. An emotional response might also be invoked – a pang of guilt if we have been delinquent; a wave of satisfaction if we had already made an advancement or had concrete plans to do so, or a sense of relief at being reminded to act.

Unless we are Operative Masons, many of the symbols in Craft Freemasonry will not routinely fall under our gaze. To fully benefit from Freemasonry's symbolism and teachings, requires our regular attendance at Lodge meetings, including any Lodges of Instruction, endeavouring to make a daily advancement of Masonic knowledge. Likewise, memorising Ritual grants 24/7 recall access whilst deepening our understanding of the core moral messages.

Symbolism works – it is visual shorthand enabling complex ideas to enjoy a sustained 'top of mind' contemplative status. By the way, never forget to:

**Note:** *Genevieve von Petzinger has published a book based on her research 'The First Signs: Unlocking the Mysteries of the World's Oldest Symbols'. ISBN 9781476785509*

# What are the Founding Grand Principles of Freemasonry?

Freemasonry is founded on three, globally accepted, moral principles – traditionally summarised as:

## Brotherly Love, Relief & Truth

In the modern idiom:

## True Friendship

## Supporting Those in Need

## Personal Integrity

In its simplest form, Freemasonry is a system of continuous self-improvement; an ongoing quest for knowledge about oneself in the context of the wider world. This is strengthened and supported by regular attendance at Lodge Meetings, where we observe or participate in Masonic Ceremonies. Both inside and outside of the Lodge we recognise designated symbols as moral mindfulness aids. In order for this to work to best effect, Masonic principles need to routinely enter our conscious thought processes. As previously mentioned, endeavouring to make a daily advancement of Masonic knowledge is strongly advocated, but not at the expense of distressing our family or working lives. In practice, 5-to 20-minutes a day adds up to a considerable advancement over time.

Masonic teachings encourage us to look inwards at ourselves to identify, consider and address any perceived weaknesses; also supporting the continuing development of our knowledge, skills and talents, both innate and those educationally acquired, for the benefit of ourselves and wider society. Likewise outwards to consider, for example, how we might best help those who are struggling to make headway in our oft troubled world.

Freemasonry is also a shared experience – by working together in fraternal friendship we strive to make the whole greater than the sum of its parts for the benefit of the wider society. Many Brethren find attending Masonic meetings to be spiritually uplifting – leaving their worldly troubles and woes outside the door of the Lodge; enjoying the good company of kindred spirits; all sharing a common, morally founded philosophy, sincerely and happily invested in the three Grand Principles above.

# What is Freemasonry Definitely Not?

**Freemasonry is not a Religion:** Membership of the Craft simply requires a belief in the existence of a Supreme Being, so it is not an imperative to subscribe to a particular religion. As a system of morality, Freemasonry does not define what is, or is not, morally acceptable behaviour. Instead, it directs us to the moral teachings enshrined in the faith or moral code we personally subscribe to and the laws of the land in which we are physically present. Many Members are drawn from recognised religions – all around the world – every Brother unified by the three Grand Principles previously explained.

**Freemasonry is not just a Fundraising Organisation:** There is a presumption in Freemasonry that every Brother innately gives freely to support those in distressed circumstances. This is subject to having the means to do so, and certainly without compromising family life. Freemasonry has a number of charitable structures to help us direct our charitable giving to best, collective effect. Masonic Charity operates at three levels, namely nationally, regionally and locally and will be considered in more detail further on.

In Freemasonry, charity is much broader than monetary giving – for example, a few well-chosen words can help lift the human spirit, inspire and motivate. There are no formal requirements for Brethren to give voluntary community service or conduct fund raising initiatives – these are matters of personal conscience, circumstances and means. However, many Masons certainly choose to do so both individually and/or collectively as a Lodge.

**Freemasonry is not a Dining Club:** Making new friends is a very welcome, natural by-product of Freemasonry but is not, in itself, a reason for joining. Festive Boards form part of the overall Lodge meeting experience; indeed, certain aspects are customarily recorded in Lodge minutes. We have laboured in the Lodge meeting and then move on to a period of refreshment which we collectively enjoy, observing customary formalities such as Masonic Toasts. Joining just for the dining experience alone risks closing the mind to Freemasonry's self-improvement benefits, greatly limiting the Masonic experience. That said, there is a world of difference between a hard working Brother with a young family needing to take a bit of a back seat for a period of time and someone who simply sees nothing more than the sociability of a good meal.

# How does Masonic Learning Develop over Time?

One might simply say that Freemasonry is a personal journey of self-discovery, which accrues over a lifetime of acquiring new knowledge, experiences and inward reflection. However, this risks the inference that after an initial induction Brethren are cut loose to make their own way. This is not the intended outcome because Freemasonry is very much a 'shared experience' based fraternity. If we ever have a sensation of feeling adrift, or a diminished sense of belonging or understanding, then we need to seek advice. Our Proposer and/or Bro Mentor would be good starting out points.

What may help our understanding is to have some real world comparisons to illustrate the progressive nature of the educational and philosophical experiences that lay ahead. For example, we can liken the three Craft Ceremonies to an accelerated primary, secondary and tertiary education.

**The First Degree – *Ceremony of Initiation* –** is largely teaching based and instruction starts as soon as the blessing of material light is restored to us, culminating with the Charge after Initiation. This Charge spells out what is expected of us – ideally, we ought to have a copy of it to reflect upon. We can liken this Degree to primary to pre-sixth form years of secondary schooling – an initial teaching centric bias that gradually introduces self-study disciplines.

**The Second Degree – *Ceremony of Passing* [Fellow Craft] –** is akin to the sixth form and tertiary education; the subject matter is more focussed, comprising a mix of teachings, but quickly skews towards a research based self-study regime.

Purely from a Masonic knowledge perspective, **The Third Degree – *Ceremony of Being Raised to the Sublime Degree of a Master Mason* –** has the feel of a Graduation Day when the surmounting of a pinnacle of Masonic knowledge is recognised. The view from the Master Mason pinnacle reveals that we are situated in the middle of a range of other opportunity peaks; some about the same height as our present situation and some higher; some are tantalisingly close and some more distant, possibly shrouded in clouds, so hiding their true form. These peaks represent our Post-Graduate opportunities and our continuing Masonic journey and are briefly summarised opposite:

**Staying put on the Master Mason's pinnacle:** It may be that we have found our optimum level of involvement that yields both happiness and satisfaction. There are no issues with this, we know our own minds which we can always change. In any event, there are so many progression opportunity pinnacles to consider, we might sensibly wish to stay put for a while to evaluate the panorama of prospects before us.

**Progressing to serve as Worshipful Master:** There are six Progressive Offices in the Lodge, culminating in serving our Lodge as its Worshipful Master. These form a line of six progressive peaks leading away from us, each gaining in height in terms of Masonic experience and knowledge – *Inner Guard, Junior Deacon, Senior Deacon, Junior Warden* and *Senior Warden* all form a progressive ridgeway of ascent. This leads us to a sixth peak, by far the highest and most distant, called *Worshipful Master*.

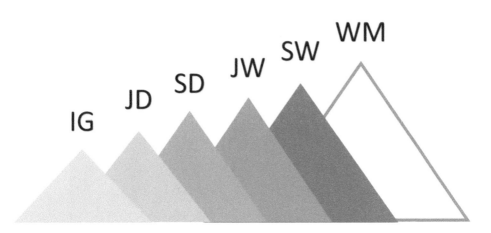

**Memorising and Presenting Ritual:** These summits are plentiful, varying in height according to the scale and complexity of the Ritual being memorised. The act of memorisation will deepen our understanding of the integral Masonic teachings and reflected in our eventual presentation of the work. Surmounting one or more of these summits will help to keep our own Lodge in a healthy, functional state. It also helps build our confidence whilst giving our mental faculties something of a healthy work out.

See Part 6 of *The New Mason's Friend* to try out a simple, scientifically founded, Ritual memorisation system.

**Other Lodge Offices:** It may well be that we have other relevant skills that could be applied to fulfilling one of the more administrative, managerial, charitable or welfare orientated Lodge Offices.

It is important to take our time in determining our future direction of Masonic travel – thus ensuring that we make the right decisions for the right reasons.

**Other Masonic Orders:** There are a goodly number of other Masonic Orders – each a pinnacle of new Masonic knowledge and symbolism, all scattered around our present location, ready and waiting to be explored. The closest to us is that of 'Royal Arch Masonry' – the black edged section of the *Book of Constitutions* deals exclusively with the Order which is also warmly referred to as 'Chapter'. It is important to ensure that we can devote enough time in order to make a proper commitment to joining something new; that our immediate family are happy for us to do so; that the dues are affordable and that our working lives will not be compromised.

**Extending our Masonic Knowledge:** There are many summits of opportunity to consider including studying Masonic history, visiting other Lodges – both in the UK and overseas, undertaking Masonic research, taking on a Masonic charity project, being an understudy and standby for a Lodge Office etc.

**Voluntary Service:** Last, but not least, let us not forget the world beyond the Lodge doors. We could become a community ambassador for Freemasonry by gifting our time and industry in voluntary service to a worthy local community group, good cause or charity.

# What are the Origins of the Word 'Freemason'?

The earliest written English references to Freemasons do not appear until the 1390s although there are some 12th century Latin references translating as 'sculptors of the free stone'.

Finer carved or shaped stone workings were fashioned out of 'Freestone' a general term for stone with a very fine grain (such as limestone and sandstone) that could be 'freely' worked in any direction. The finest freestone can even be cut with a saw.

Many in the wider non-Masonic academic world accept the definition of Freemason to be a skilled Mason who can competently work freestone into a desired form; a Mason who expertly finesses the stone with a chisel rather than a lowlier skilled Mason who renders the stone into rough blocks with an axe or hammer. The latter group were historically known as 'Rough Masons' or 'Row Masons'. However, all Masons learnt the basic 'shaping' skills first.

*Within the Masonic universe there are a number of other explanations:*

Many Brethren believe this to be the most likely origin: Following the Norman Conquest, the demand for Stone Masons boomed resulting in French Masons crossing the Channel in search of work. So, there exists a highly plausible

French connection with 'Franc-Maçons' (Free-Masons). In some contexts, the French word 'franc' means 'free' – Wikipedia cites 'coup franc' as such an example – French for a 'free kick' in footballing parlance. In medieval France, Franc-Maçons worked on religious buildings, enjoying the dual privileges of their wages being free from taxation and their labours free from interference by local officials.

The official language of the post Conquest English royal court was Norman French and did not change to English until 1399 when Henry IV acceded the throne. This seems to chime with the first written references to Freemasons in English not appearing before the 1390s. It is also possible that the skilled 'Franc-Maçons' worked predominantly on large scale ecclesiastical projects and were protected (free) to some extent from being conscripted (called 'Impressment') by the King to undertake urgent, but usually more lowly skilled, castle building work.

Finally, some Brethren consider that a Freemason is a Mason who did not hold membership of a Guild, so was 'free' of the Guild. There were certainly independent medieval Masons who worked as local jobbing builders, but they tended to work on small scale jobs, some working as quarrymen when masonry work was scarce.

A little further on, we will also see that the 'freedom' to work as a Mason in a large township or city was highly regulated.

Figure of Henry IV
within York Minster

**Note:** *The word 'free' occurs in two other Masonic contexts namely as a 'freeman' and 'free and accepted or speculative'. Both usages are explained in the next question.*

# What are the Contextual Meanings of the Word 'Free'?

Having considered how the name 'Freemason' came into the English language, we can now look at two other applications of the word 'Free' namely:

- **Freeman or Free man**

- **Free and Accepted, or Speculative**

Both feature in the Ceremony of Initiation.

**Freeman:** Post 1066, under the medieval Feudal System, the Peasantry were split into several sub-classes of Serfdom – all but one was tied by contract to the land held under tenure by their Feudal Lords. The one exception were Freemen who typically rented or leased agricultural land, which they worked for a profit on a self-employed basis. Not being tied to the land, Freemen were thus free to travel. The children of Freemen, likewise free to travel, were therefore eligible to take on a trade or merchant apprenticeship in a market town or city.

Unwittingly taking on an apprentice from any other class of the Peasantry usually ended disastrously for the Master concerned. Once discovered, the Feudal Lord simply reasserted his rights which were contractually superior to those invested in the apprenticeship contract. It mattered not a jot if the youth was in his final, seventh year of apprenticeship!

Young Serfs sometimes ran away to a large town or city hoping to secure employment or an apprenticeship by pretending to be 'free born'. Masters and their Guilds would be particularly vigilant in this regard, but we know that some were seduced by a well contrived tale.

**Freeman of a Town:** Completing a market town Guild apprenticeship usually conferred the privilege of being made a Freeman of that town. Guildhalls also functioned as local councils in addition to hosting Merchant and Trade Guild meetings. This 'freedom' afforded certain rights such as being 'free' to practise a trade within a defined geographical area.

**Accepted Mason:** By the early 17th century men of wealth and position were paying to join Operative Lodges as non-operative members – they were 'accepted' as being equal to operative members. Following the formation of premier Grand Lodge in 1717, non-operative Lodge members were formally described as 'Free and Accepted Masons'.

**Speculative Masons:** By the middle of the same century the term 'Speculative' was likewise applied to certain non-operative members – the use of mathematics in creating building designs did not require the use of physical tools, but

rather utilised those of the mind. Such knowledge based design processes employed, for example, by an architect were 'Speculative'.

**King's College Chapel, Cambridge:** Has the largest fan vaulted ceiling in the world. The Master Mason architect John Wastell, took just three years to complete the work between 1512-1515. A brilliant example of stunning 'speculative' design from the mind of a great medieval architect.

**Summary:** 'Free, Accepted or Speculative Masons' are all non-operative Lodge members, accorded the same freedoms and privileges as their 'Operative' counterparts, without the need to serve a formal 7 year apprenticeship.

# How Far Back in Time does Freemasonry Date Itself?

We are all familiar with multiple choice examination type questions, but in Freemasonry some questions have multiple answers, some have one and many have none at all! In this instance there are three, revolving around a Calendar, Historical Setting and origins of our present day Craft Ceremonies.

**1]**    **Masonic Calendar:  Anno Lucis** [AL] 'The year of light' is an 18th century dating system, predominantly used in Freemasonry, that is similar to the Hebrew calendar **Anno Mundi** 'Year after creation'. Both use biblical references to date the creation of the world and the time of Adam – taken to have occurred 4,000 years BCE. So, the Gregorian Calendar year of 2020 CE equates to 6020 AL – 6020 years after the creation of the world.

**2]**    **Historical Setting of Masonic Ceremonies:  King Solomon's Temple** [KST]: Masonic mythology has it that Adam passed the principles of Masonry down through the generations to the builders of KST. Our Masonic Craft Ceremony story lines are accordingly set at the time of KST's construction in Jerusalem, the commencement of building works is broadly accepted as having been around BCE 967 or AL 3033. Biblical references state that it took Solomon 7 years to complete the Temple.

KST is also known as 'The First Temple' due to its destruction by fire more than four centuries after its completion, following the Siege of Jerusalem in BCE 587. It was subsequently replaced by 'The Second Temple' completed about 70 years later, c. BCE 517. Neither temple physically exists today, nor does any faithful image of their exterior or interior forms. Partial descriptions of The First Temple are recorded in both the Jewish and Christian bibles.

**3]**    **Masonic Craft Ceremonies:** Although Craft Freemasonry dates itself back to the Year of Light and the subsequent building of KST, the present day Ceremony of Initiation is accepted as taking its rise from those practised by the Medieval Masons Guilds of the 13th to 15th centuries. It is also possible that the origins of some of its parts may go back much further – for the want of written records, we simply do not know. There have also been a number of much later additions such as the application of physical penalties. In *Part 3* of *The New Mason's Friend* we will tour through the whole Ceremony of Initiation pointing out some of its medieval themes.

# What did Medieval Guilds Contribute to Freemasonry?

We can look back to the early days of the Roman Kingdom (founded c. 753 BCE) where many groups, including the majority of trades, formed voluntary collegiate styled bodies (Collegia) to represent members' interests. European medieval merchants recreated the Collegia concept from the 11th century in the form of Guilds. Initially established in major cities, Guilds rapidly grew in number, expanding their reach to include all manner of trades and vocations. They established themselves as Companies, Corporations, Colleges, Societies, Fraternities, Brotherhoods etc.

Each Guild set the rules and professional standards for the guidance and compliance of its members – ensuring their enforcement, inspecting workmanship and adjudicating over complaints and grievances. By the 15th century a Guild was also referred to as a Mistery, derived from the old French word 'mestier' (modern 'metier') which simply means 'trade'. The present day 'Mysteries or Misteries of Freemasonry' are sometimes taken to allude to trade secrets, but this rather presumes there were any.

Guilds also conducted Ceremonies of Initiation for new Apprentices; maintained a register of members and their Degree qualifications and collected membership fees and fines. The Guilds prospered, establishing their own market town- and city-based meeting halls; creating colourful and impactful livery (regalia) for members to wear.

The London Masons' Company (Guild) was established sometime between 1356 to 1376; its regulations (called Ordinances) having been approved in 1356. There are written references to the London Masons' Company in this context and several bequests from deceased members to 'the fraternity of my art'. Bequests sometimes included the benefactor's livery cloak – the 'regalia' of the day.

Some of the most experienced (and commercially successful) Guild members were selected and formally obligated to oversee the proper administration of their Guild's Ordinances; the most experienced masons were also permitted to take on and train Apprentices as their Masters. The Guild also appointed Wardens to monitor regulatory compliance for example, inspecting construction works for 'false masonry' – work improperly conducted – possibly by Masons not holding membership of a recognised Guild.

The Guild hierarchy evolved over time to include the offices of Worshipful Master, Wardens, Scribe (Secretary) Treasurer, Almoner and Chaplain.

In Scotland 'Corporations' were established as Guild type institutions, but with one important difference. Some of the Masons' Corporations also admitted members from other allied trades such as carpentry etc. Operative Masons (who were generally considered to be secretive) established their own fraternal Lodges, closely linked to their Masons' Corporation, purely to conduct private Masonic business, such as the Initiation of Apprentices, deal with the welfare of members etc.

The chartering of English and Welsh market towns in the 13th and 14th centuries usually incorporated Guild rules giving rise to the building of many Guild Halls. However, outside of the major towns and cities it appears that some provincial Masons did not embrace Guild membership, instead maintaining the status of independent, self-employed local jobbing builders. In the late 14th and 15th centuries, some of these Masons may have formed small fraternal groups perhaps populated by a Master's sons and nephews.

When not hosting an official meeting, Guild Halls were used for other purposes such as social entertainments and gatherings of the townsfolk. Working collectively, the early Guilds also organised civic duties such as street cleaning, night watch services and feeding the poor – they were effectively the forerunners of our local Councils.

Whilst late medieval city based Freemasons would have been Guild Members some, in order to maximise their commercial prospects, would also have been enrolled for Citizenship at the beginning of their apprenticeships (from where we derive the present day City & Guilds qualifications). Taking London as an example, there were just three routes to securing Citizenship:

- Patriarchal inheritance

- Purchasing the privilege (very expensive)

- Successfully completing a Guild apprenticeship

**Note:** *There were a small number of trades recruiting female apprentices*

**Note:** *Apprenticeship afforded the children of freemen a real opportunity for social and economic advancement.*

**Citizenship** conferred special privileges including the exclusive **'freedom'** to bid for work within the City limits. As the guilds also fulfilled a Local Government role, Citizen Masons consequently got all the best civic building jobs. Everyone else, irrespective of being born in London or not, was a 'Foreigner' unless they hailed from overseas in which case they were classified as 'Aliens'. In the late medieval period, it is estimated that Citizens accounted for no more than 12% of London's population – a Citizen Mason would have enjoyed the height of respectability as a successful businessman making a very good living. So, we have Citizen Masons and Foreigner Masons; the former group are free to bid for all the best jobs and the latter get what is left or work on a less profitable, subcontracted basis.

Citizen and Foreigner Masons were constantly at loggerheads over several centuries – the latter arguing vehemently by petitioning the King for a levelling of the commercial playing field – the former arguing, just as fiercely, that such a levelling would result in a reduction of building quality.

Guilds also functioned as welfare organisations which, as the Freemasons of today, we would instantly identify with. They provided:

- Welfare support for poorer, ill or injured Guild members and their immediate family members.

- Promotion and maintenance support of members' moral standards.

- Charitable support within their local community – helping widows, orphans and funding marriage dowries for poor girls etc.

- Reinforcement of their faith in God, for example by funding stained glass windows and the public performance of religious plays which, on occasion, they actively participated in. It is possible that the latter were the forerunners of today's Speculative Ceremonies.

**Note:** *The essence of these virtues remain at the heart of Freemasonry today, forming the three founding grand principles of **Brotherly Love**, **Relief** and **Truth**.*

The Guilds also advocated educating young people. Previously, schooling had been the preserve of the church and the exceptionally wealthy. For example, Grammar Schools were originally established to teach Latin to aspiring priests. At the beginning of the 13th century nearly everyone was illiterate; maths was limited to basic counting (using tally sticks) and 'hands-on' apprenticeships tended to start at the age of 13 years.

Two centuries later and apprenticeships generally started from the age of 15 years; some trades (apparently not Masonry) extending the apprenticeship term up to 10 years or longer to give Masters more time to recoup their investments. From the age of 12 years, many 15th century Candidates would have been taught basic reading, writing and bookkeeping skills. We know this because there are accounts of Apprentices (various trades) not only being able to recite their Obligations from memory, but also able to record them in writing. This uplift in education was in some part due to the ability of Guilds to keep the wages of the time at such a level that members had enough surplus income to school their children.

Such was the control of the Guilds, that no one could set up shop in any large town or city without belonging to the relevant Guild. The number of Masters for any one trade was geographically limited by the Guild to avoid excessive supply. However, famine, disease and unforeseen economic shocks were omnipresent often resulting in sudden falls in labour supply for all trades. Having plenty of healthy Apprentices and aspiring Masters on the books helped to provide some 'troubled times' contingency insurance to bolster the supply of skilled labour and a healthy membership headcount.

**The Old Market Hall in Shrewsbury** built in 1596. Venerable guild and market halls were often held aloft on wooden stilts or stone columns to provide privacy. Early to mid medieval buildings had a space between the eaves and the walls allowing curious 'eavesdroppers' to monitor conversations within the building. There has been a market house or hall on the Shrewsbury site since the 1260s.

# How do Operative and Speculative Freemasonry differ?

**Historically:** An Operative Mason was a qualified Stone Mason who worked the stone with physical, handheld tools. An example of medieval Speculative Masonry would have been visualising or sketching a geometrical design for an ornate window mullion. The former is a tangible product of physical labour, the latter, an envisaged product of the mind.

**Present day Operative Freemasonry:** The term 'Operative Mason' is now broadly applied to describe Brethren who work (or have worked) in a construction related profession, such as that of a qualified Civil Engineer, Master Builder, Architect, Stone Mason etc.

**Present day Speculative Freemasonry:** The practice of philosophically applying established Masonic teachings directed at self-improvement and a better understanding of the world. This is conducted by employing the cinema of the mind stimulated by allegories, symbols etc.

An **Operative Freemason** is given a block of roughly cut stone and requested to work it to form a perfect cube. Our Mason applies a hammer or axe to initially knock off the rough bits (superfluous knobs and excrescences) to crudely form the edges, regularly measuring the work with a ruler, compasses etc. to ensure a faithful progression towards the formation of a perfect cube. Thereafter, other tools such as a chisel, are used to smooth and finesse the stone's surfaces to a sensory and visually perceived state of perfection, validated by trying (gauging) each surface with a square and compasses.

A **Speculative Freemason** might, for example, take the unworked stone block to represent their own flaws and imperfections, after all, as mere mortals none of us are without them. Thinking about improving such matters may bring to the fore something that the Brother would like to address – perhaps an elderly relative they have not spoken with for some time springs to mind. Thought processes might move on to consider how the relative feels about the absence of communication triggering some overdue remedial action.

In Freemasonry, the unworked stone is called the *Rough Ashlar;* taken directly from the quarry it represents someone in an uneducated and uncultured state.

The worked upon *Perfect Ashlar,* which is ready to build with, represents someone cultivated, educated and refined.

The Rough Ashlar also represents us as Entered Apprentices, at the very beginning of our Masonic life journey with little in the way of Masonic knowledge, whilst a Master Mason is represented by the Perfect Ashlar.

Recognising that absolute perfection is beyond the reach of us as mere mortals, the Perfect Ashlar can also allude to the Supreme Being.

# How Did Operative Masonry Evolve?

Monks were the predominant stonemasons and builders of the early to mid-medieval period – the earliest works were expedited by monastic orders, such as the Benedictines. Several of these orders used signs as a preferred means of communication. There were no 'vows of silence' as such – it was simply accepted that silence or limited conversation kept the airwaves open to hear the voice of God, so minimising the risk of sinning. Construction sites could also be very noisy making verbal communication, over even a short distance, somewhat difficult. Some Masonic scholars believe several of those early signs continue to be used in Craft Freemasonry today. Under the tutelage of the monks, local labourers gained enough masonry knowhow to set up small family businesses or fraternities – the local builders of their day.

Following the founding of the first cathedral in Canterbury in 597 several others followed over the ensuing 150 years – in London (604) Rochester (604) Winchester (650) Lichfield (669) Hereford (676) Worcester (743). By the end of the first millennium groups of Masons were touring the countryside offering stone built parish churches of a standard design. There were at least 30 English stone built monasteries, ranging from Cornwall to Cumbria, all operating as self-contained economic centres.

After the Norman Conquest in 1066, Odo confronted those who continued to resist the rule of his brother, William the Conqueror. By 1072 any notion of continuing rebellion had been quelled and William's opponents, many of whom fled into exile, had their lands confiscated. William redistributed these lands to his most loyal supporters.

Both the Crown and the Church physically proclaimed their newfound power via the landscapes of England and Wales. Their large scale construction of stone built castles, palaces, monasteries and cathedrals etc continue to dominate the landscape of today. Whilst the Crown commissioned many castles, by far the largest masonry client was the Church commissioning works including humble parish churches, monasteries, hospitals, grammar schools, colleges, and cathedrals of awe inspiring, breath-taking proportions. This created a formidable demand for Masons, other allied trades, materials and, most importantly of all, those truly exceptionally gifted Master Mason architects sufficiently skilled to design the buildings and oversee the construction works.

The most challenging and ornate work was invested in the construction of cathedrals – a mission of the highest order with the remit to 'create heaven on earth'. By the late 11th century some 15 cathedrals were under construction resulting in an influx of Masons from overseas, most notably from France.

By 1180 a new Gothic style of cathedral architecture had been imported from France succeeding the traditional Romanesque forms, the latter distinguished by their more rustic design features and rounded arches.

***Early English Gothic*** architecture was characterised by its high vaulted roofs, towering spires, wall supporting flying buttresses and stunning stone arches and windows which tapered, with mesmerising symmetry, to a fine point. This architectural form, offering a superior distribution of weight and centres of gravity, allowed 'The Master Mason' architects of the day to think wider, longer and higher.

*Early English Gothic 'Scissor Arch' in Wells Cathedral.*
*The cathedral was built between 1176 -1450*

The pinnacle of any Mason's career was being appointed The Master Mason (architect) of a major construction project such as a Cathedral. All the other masons and trades, such as carpenters, roofers, glaziers, lead workers and tilers worked under his direct control. In practice, for larger scale projects, he would have appointed a Clerk of Works to assist with the day-to-day management of the site and its personnel. He also liaised with the building's patron, usually an eminent cleric or crown appointed official.

**Note:** *The title of 'The Master Mason' should not be confused with the Degree qualification of Master Mason in Speculative Freemasonry*

Any Master Mason appointed to design and build a cathedral would have been very well educated, most likely from a family of high social standing and widely travelled scrutinising many noteworthy buildings to help inspire and shape their own ideas. It is very obvious from the abundance of Cathedral design similarities that The Master Mason architects freely shared their architectural concepts and seemed happy for these to be copied. It seems highly plausible that, later on in history, Master Mason architects contributed to the creation and establishment of Speculative Freemasonry.

It is interesting to note that prior to the establishment of the London Masons' Company, 'Apprentices' are not mentioned in either Church, or Crown buildings financial accounts. The considered view is that the basic skills were then simply passed on to sons, nephews, quarrymen and Masons' servants (labourers) aspiring to improve their circumstances by learning on the job. There are very early records of Cistercian monks paying experienced Masons to teach their skills to younger men. Later financial accounts show that Entered Apprentices were sometimes accorded a fractional wage which varied according to their abilities – this wage was most likely paid directly to the Master who may have passed some of it on as pocket money.

This meant that both the Crown and Church, as the major masonry clients of the time, held the economic power to either control or very heavily influence Masons' wages. This was counterbalanced, to some large extent, by the Guilds fulfilling a trade union like negotiating role. It is also clear from the buildings accounts of the time that Masons received wages according to their ability, consequently there were numerous skill based 'rates of pay' variations.

Given that Cathedral build times could be as long as 80 years, lifetime contracts were taken up by some Masons. It is unlikely that Guilds would have approved of these – did you need to be a member if you had a job for life?

Finally, both the Crown, and the Church under licence from the Crown, could Impress (legally compel) Masons to go and work for the King's wage on any building where rapid construction was deemed an imperative. Over a two year period (1360-1363) Edward III ordered several waves of Impressment for Masons to work on rebuilding the palace at Windsor Castle. Unfortunately, the Masons were dying from the plague in considerable number, so the Impressment net was forever being cast further afield.

Ultimately around 30 Shire County Sheriffs Impressed more than 1,650 Masons and Layers (Masons who laid and set worked stones with lime based mortar) the final wave taking men from Devon, Hereford, Shropshire, Derbyshire, Nottinghamshire, Lancashire and Yorkshire.

To afford some scale of headcount context, in 1377, the entire population of London was estimated to be around just 40,000.

Imagine trying to enforce such an arrangement today!

So, the Guilds, later to become known as Misteries, took root, flourishing in the 13th to 15th centuries with Masonry operating as a highly regarded, morally principled, regulated trade.

**Windsor Castle:** *Originally a largely wooden castle built by William the Conqueror c. 1070. Converted to a stone built fortified palace by Henry II in the late 12th century.*

*Edward III rebuilt the palace in Gothic form 1350-77.*

# What is the Earliest Recorded Masonic Document?

**King Athelstan, c. 894 to 939:** Athelstan was the grandson of Alfred the Great, reigning as King of the Anglo Saxons from 924. He was not crowned until the following year due to resistance from Wessex which was quelled within a matter of months. In 927 he reconquered the last Viking stronghold in York which meant he could be fairly proclaimed 'King of the English' and this second reign ran from 927 to his death in 939. Athelstan also gained control over Scotland in 934 when his invasion forces compelled Constantine II to submit to him.

Many modern historians now regard Athelstan to be the most learned of the Anglo Saxon kings – he reformed the law; created a highly effective central government machine; built strong relationships with European monarchs; he was very pious (an enthusiastic collector of religious relics) and consequently highly supportive of church and monastic building developments. Like his grand-father, he too proved to be a fervent educationalist and drew many scholars to his court. It is this point that interests Masons because there are references to Athelstan in Freemasonry's oldest surviving document, the Regius Poem, which is presently housed in The British Museum.

The Regius Poem was initially dated from c. 1390, but is now considered to date between 1425 to 1450. According to some specialist linguists, the poem is thought be a copy of a much older document, possibly originally scribed in the county of Shropshire. The heart of the poem describes the moral and working duties of Master Masons (15 Articles – some dealing with Apprentices) which we might call *'Old Charges'* and similarly for Craftsmen (qualified Masons) with 15 Points to contemplate. The behavioural advice on offer ranges from not committing murder to exercising good table manners, including how to sneeze when in polite company. There are numerous references to the management of Apprentices.

Most importantly of all, the Regius Poem describes how Euclid's proof of Pythagoras's Theorem entered English Masonry during the reign of King Athelstan. Legend has it that the Masons of the time approached Athelstan to help them form the Charges for the proper governance of Masonry. On the opposite page, there is an extract from the poem in modern English language:

*In time of good King Athelstane's day;*
*He made then both hall and even bower,*
*And high temples of great honour,*
*To disport him in both day and night,*
*And to worship his God with all his might.*
*This good lord loved this craft full well,*
*And purposed to strengthen it every part,*
*For various faults that in the craft he found;*
*He sent about into the land*

*After all the masons of the craft,*
*To come to him full even straight,*
*For to amend these defaults all*
*By good counsel, if it might fall.*
*An assembly then could let make*
*Of various lords in their state,*

*Dukes, earls, and barons also,*
*Knights, squires and many more,*
*And the great burgesses of that city*
*They were there all in their degree;*
*There were there each one always*
*To ordain for these masons' estate*
*There they sought by their wit,*
*How they might govern it;*

*Fifteen articles they there sought,*
*And fifteen points there they wrought,*

The poem comprises 64 pages of vellum detailing 794 lines in rhyming couplet form. Given the great oral tradition of the times, the rhyming nature would have made the poem easier to memorise, either in full or part.

**Note:** *'Bower' is either a retreat or a Lady's private apartment in a medieval hall.*

Whilst historians generally accept that the *Regius Poem* is actually a copy of a much older document, there are two later, similarly modelled, manuscripts purporting to offer a more detailed account of events:

- **The Matthew Cooke Manuscript** – written 1450s
  second oldest Masonic Document

- **The Lansdowne Manuscript** – written around 1560

Taken as a whole, the three manuscripts subsequently gave rise to 'The Legend of York'. The basic premise is that the very first Grand Lodge was formed in York around 926 when King Athelstan's brother, Prince Edwin organised a General Assembly of Masons. They approved a Constitution, as described in the Regius Poem. This notion has occupied many Masonic minds questing to prove or disprove the legend – at the present time the status of 'legend' is maintained.

We will briefly return to the Legend of York, as much later on it plays a role in the formation of the United Grand Lodge of England.

**Note:** *The* Book of Constitutions, *pages 143 to 150, details the present day Charges of a Free Mason*

*Figure of King Athelstan at Ripon Cathedral – we are meant to infer from the scroll in his right hand that he was a man of great learning and wisdom.*

# Did Medieval Masons Live in Lodges?

A medieval Mason's Lodge was not how we now know it today – effectively a meeting room, but rather refers to the workshop erected at the construction site, quarry or possibly forming part of a Master Mason's trade premises. The typical Lodge was an open sided, lean-to affair, usually made from planks of pinewood with a thatched roof. On construction sites, Lodges were usually set against a principal wall of the main building which served as a wind break cum shelter. Although single storey, some Lodges included a loft space for the storage of tools and materials. Despite the name, there was no residential usage although some of our early Brethren would most likely have taken their official 30 minute summer afternoon nap in the shade of the Lodge canopy.

On large scale building projects, Lodges would be established at the quarry – here Masons would work the larger stones into a near finished, lighter form for ease of transportation. Stones, both worked and unworked, were transported from the quarry to the construction site by oxcart, raft or boat. Small villages would have sprung up around both the large scale construction site and the nearby quarry to accommodate workers and their families.

Our Operative forebears had very long working hours, up to 16 hours a day in the summer months. Masons' working hours were often specified as being at the workplace (the Lodge) half an hour before sunrise to half an hour after sunset – presumably the 30 minutes at beginning and end of the day were to allow for readying, tidying and praying. There were several official breaks including that half hour summer nap!

Medieval buildings accounts often disclose that there were differing summer and winter day rates of pay, the latter being somewhat lower reflecting the relative shortness of the solar day. Masons who specialised in setting the stonework, called 'Layers' were usually laid off or redeployed in the damper winter months as the lime based mortar needed summer warmth to set.

With the passing of time, Lodges became more refined becoming fully enclosed, tiled and better suited to the holding of private meetings.

Lodges evolved from these humble buildings to the customised Lodge Rooms of today. Make no mistake, both were designed for labour; the former for Operative Masonry and the latter for contemplative moralisation invoked by the ceremonies and symbols of Speculative Freemasonry.

# How did Speculative Freemasonry Evolve?

The honest answer is that we cannot be certain for the want of records, but such a change clearly evolved through a number of stages:

- Guilds weakened to a point where they no longer exerted influence, so we need to consider the factors that contributed to this outcome
- The economic factors that encouraged the formation of independent Masons' Lodges
- The catalysts triggering the admission of 'speculative members' who had neither operative skill, nor any desire to serve a 7-year operative apprenticeship

Below is a summary of some of the contributory factors that collectively weakened Guilds' authority from 1500 to 1700:

- **High Inflation:** The discovery of the Americas resulted in the import of precious metals, chiefly silver, into those European countries with an Atlantic coastline, most notably Spain. There was a lot of import trade from China at the time; Chinese merchants would only accept payment in silver. Consequently, the value of silver rose causing significant price inflation throughout the civilised world.

- **Wage Stagnation:** From 1361 to 1530, the wages paid to Masons employed at Oxford, Cambridge and London Bridge stagnated, but over the same period the price of food increased by a third. Between 1501 to 1702 wages increased by nearly 350% but food prices had risen by nearly 700%, double the rate of wage inflation. From the 16th century it seems that the Guilds exerted little or no influence over wages with Masonry's principal clients – the Crown, Church and Civic Authorities all seemingly dictating rates of pay.

- **Henry VIII – Dissolution of the Monasteries:** Some 900 monastic estates, considerably varying in size, collectively controlled around 25% of England's landmass. These vibrant economic centres were constantly extending and rebuilding their estate infrastructures, employing a goodly number of Masons. They and thousands of other workers lost their livelihoods. The process of Dissolution started in 1536; by 1540 Monasteries were closing at the approximate rate of one per week.

In the main, Henry sold the Monasteries to the highest bidders who often proceeded to dismantle the buildings and dispose of or redeploy the redundant masonry. This supply of low cost recycled stone effectively shut down all the quarries simultaneously weakening the Masons' Guilds.

**Note***: it would be a disservice not to mention the considerable loss of Monastic support for the destitute and the sick – a point that would not have been lost on our Operative forebears.*

- **Small is Beautiful:** In smaller settlements, independent Masons (known as Small Masters – perhaps one Master Mason and an Apprentice) or small, informal Fraternities fulfilled the role of local jobbing builders. They undertook commissions for minor building works, repairs and making utility pieces such as the Creeing Trough opposite. Most Small Masters worked not for wages, but for fees negotiated directly with

**Medieval Creeing Trough:** *Carved from stone and used as a mortar in which grain was 'creed' (pounded) to remove husks.*

their customers. Consequently, they were better insulated from the ravages of price inflation then their wage earning peers. This most likely would not have escaped the attention of wage earning Masons.

- **Diminishing Demand for Church Building:**
The cathedral building period was now long past; the demand for stone built parish churches, being broadly sated by 1500, meant many Masons had to content themselves with ecclesiastical building maintenance and repair works. There was relatively very little new church building in the 16th century.

- **Diminishing Demand from the Crown:** Whilst royal palace and castle building and rebuilding works continued apace during the reign of Henry VIII, demand was somewhat more muted during the Elizabethan period. The first English deployment of cannons is considered to have been near Crecy in 1346 during the early stages of the Hundred Years War. Thereafter, it took a long time for cannon technology to evolve into an effective, lightweight, manoeuvrable, long range form.

By the 16th century lightweight cannon would easily demolish stone built castles and city walls which considerably dampened defensive stone construction demand. Queen Elizabeth I, fearing an invasion from Scotland, spent a considerable sum fortifying the border, most notably in Berwick-upon-Tweed. There, new cannon proof defences were deployed utilising an array of 50 feet wide, 30 feet high, earth banks secreting batteries of cannons set up in a supremely defensive crossfire system. Taking 10 years to complete, there was hardly any masonry work involved – mainly requiring a large army of wheelbarrow pushing, shovel bearing labourers.

*Earthen banked, cannon proof fortifications at Berwick-upon-Tweed commissioned by Elizabeth I. Secreting cross-firing cannon batteries – the very high cost 'Trident' defensive system of the day.*

- **Union of the Crowns:** The Union of the Crowns by marriage in 1603 ushered in a period of relative peace with the Crown's, nobility's and gentry's need for fortified buildings consequently diminishing.

- **Building with Bricks:** Brick construction became increasingly popular throughout the period – indeed with the exception of churches, most of the houses lost in the Great Fire of London in 1666 were rebuilt using bricks and tiles for roofing.

Many individuals prospered from the discovery of the Americas and eventually some of this wealth found its way into the domestic economy. A rising demand from the burgeoning gentry to build, rebuild or extend country halls, more in keeping with a more ornate European style, presented Masons with a growing but fragmented private market opportunity. The spectrum of new European design features even included black and white square floor tiles! It is therefore not beyond the realms of imagination to see Masonic businesses (Lodges) exploring how best to meet this rising tide of private sector demand.

Securing work would have either required some form of outreach networking or an approach from agents on behalf of the gentry. In such an environment, it can be readily envisaged that the most skilled and accomplished Masons' Lodges would wish to form close, enduring relationships with the higher orders of the gentry to help promote their commercial interests. Ultimately, some of the gentry may have been offered the opportunity of becoming Accepted Freemasons, to extend the social networking reach of Lodges.

The switch in demand for stone masonry from the church and crown to a more fragmented private sector created a positive, economic environment for Speculative Freemasonry to take root in. It is generally accepted that Speculative Freemasonry was the invention of a liberally minded, enlightened group of men seeking to heal the divisions of a challenged world through a new philosophical approach. This line of thinking resonates very well with that of the Renaissance movement. Recognising the teachings of the Christian Bible enjoyed a near universal understanding – they took the construction of King Solomon's Temple – the oldest building mentioned in the Old Testament – to serve as their new philosophy's principal metaphor. To bring their concept into early reality required the initial collaboration of one or more Operative Lodges willing to share their own insights, heritage and moral values.

As stated at the outset, we do not really know for certain how Speculative Freemasonry evolved either out of, or in collaboration with, the Operative dynamic. However, there were very powerful moral, economic and social arguments for such an evolution, which continues to be highly valued today by the global fraternity that is Speculative Freemasonry.

# Who was the first recorded Speculative Freemason in England?

*Elias Ashmole*: was the first recorded English Speculative Freemason to be Initiated in England. As a widower, who found himself on the losing 'Loyalist' side of the English Civil War, Elias Ashmole went to live in Cheshire with his father-in-law, Peter Mainwaring.

He was Initiated into the Lodge of Lights in Warrington on 4th October 1646 at 4.30pm. We know this with exactitude because he recorded the details in his diary also stating that he was 'made a Free-Mason with Coll. Henry Mainwaring of Karincham in Cheshire', another close family member.

Ashmole even listed the names of the other Lodge members in attendance, most of whom appear not to have been Operative stone masons.

This discloses two points of historical merit:

- That 'Accepted' membership existed some time before the Initiation of Elias Ashmole in 1646 – clearly some of the local gentry were already Accepted members of the Lodge of Lights. Such earlier admissions were reinforced to some extent by the 1620/21 Record Book of the London Masons' Company. This recorded the term 'The Acception' which appears to refer to a group of non-operative Masons attached to the Company.

- Henry Mainwaring was a Parliamentarian and Elias Ashmole, a relatively high ranking Loyalist. This juxtaposition is taken to be the earliest example of Freemasonry's non-acceptance of political division. The township of Warrington had been staunchly Parliamentarian throughout the civil war; notwithstanding, Elias Ashmole was seemingly welcomed into Freemasonry there without any hint of political prejudice. Had there been, he would have likely noted it in his diary.

Freemasonry seems to have marked a positive turning point in Ashmole's life. Having re-established himself in London society (thanks in some measure to Freemasonry) and fulfilling his diarised ambition of remarrying into wealth, he later gifted a display of curios to Oxford University, providing the foundations for the later establishment of the Ashmolean Museum.

# Why did Freemasonry 'Go Quiet' in World War II?

The simple answer is that the Nazi regime outlawed Freemasonry claiming it was very strongly linked to the Jewry and had therefore contributed to Germany losing World War I. When the regime came to power, it urged domestic Freemasons to give up their Masonic memberships. In January 1933 Hermann Goering decreed that Lodges should voluntarily dissolve, officially submitting their plans to do so for his approval. In early 1934, the judiciary decreed that those Masons who had not already left the Craft by the 30th January 1933, were unable to join the Nazi Party. The summer of the same year, the police were ordered to forcibly close Masonic Lodges and their administrative centres confiscating documents, libraries and artefacts.

Considerable pressures resulted in a much reduced German Freemasonry going underground as many Masons lost their jobs. Freemasons were banned from certain forms of employment with an omnipresent risk of being kept under surveillance and even falling victim to indiscriminate physical violence. Consequently, later in the war there ensued a labour shortage resulting in a softening of domestic stance, but it came at the price of Masonic jobseekers renouncing Freemasonry during a period of amnesty.

Masonic Lodges in Nazi occupied countries were raided, their property and documents (including membership lists) were all confiscated. Anti-Freemasonry exhibitions, violent oppression, arrests as political opponents and detention in concentration camps were commonplace. As some German Freemasons were of the Jewish faith it is not possible to say how many Freemasons of all faiths were murdered under the Nazi regime – estimates run as high as 200,000.

Before the outbreak of World War II, British Freemasonry had been quite open, with Freemasons generally held in high regard for their charitable undertakings. It was not at all unusual for Freemasons to parade through the streets with other social groups on special civic occasions, or to have official presence during the laying of foundation stones of public buildings. With the invasion of Britain in prospect, and knowledge of the Reich's treatment of Masons in occupied countries, British Freemasonry understandably went quiet. In a very uncertain post-war climate it inclined to stay that way, arguably for far too long. However, what follows overleaf evinces the irrepressible nature of the Masonic spirit when confronted with adversity:

**Forget-me-not Flower:** You may have seen Brethren wearing a forget-me-not flower lapel pin (or indeed already own one) and wondered about its significance. The flower is an internationally accepted Masonic 'identification' symbol and some Brethren wear it outside of the Lodge for this reason. It also serves to remind us of the love of Freemasonry in times of great duress when the resilience of the human spirit comes to the fore.

Three key events gave rise to the symbolic adoption of the forget-me-not:

1. 1n 1926 the forget-me-not was adopted as an emblem for the annual meeting of the United Grand Lodge of Germany, held in Brennan. A local factory manufactured and supplied a lapel pin.

2. As previously mentioned, in 1934 legislation came into force effectively resulting in the dissolution of Freemasonry in Nazi Germany; membership and meetings were banned, Masonic property confiscated, and some Brethren were detained as political prisoners of the Third Reich. The same draconian measures were vigorously applied in other Nazi controlled countries including Vichy France, Italy, Belgium etc.

3. In 1933, Hitler also decreed the banning of all private charities – establishing in their stead a single Nazi controlled welfare organisation, the Nationalsozialistische Volkswohlfahrt, or NSV [National Socialist People's Welfare Organization]. At its height, the NSV supported 19 million German citizens, organising many national fundraising events including the Winterhilfswerk, or Winter Support Programme. In 1938, by pure happenchance, winter programme organisers chose a forget-me-not flower lapel pin as a gift to donors – actually commissioning the pins from the very same factory that had supplied the Grand Lodge of Germany some 12 years earlier.

Thus, the forget-me-not flower became a Nazi backed social welfare symbol that could also be openly worn by Freemasons, communicating their membership of the Craft. No doubt, it was worn with some considerable measure of caution, surpassed by a superior sense of pride.

Caution should be exercised when encountering someone sporting such a lapel pin badge outside of the Lodge environment.

Best to first enquire of the wearer the pin's significance. For example, the forget-me-not is also the national flower of the US State of Alaska, and more recently in the UK, has been adopted as a symbol of dementia.

**Loge Liberté Chérie:** There are records of seven Belgium Masonic political prisoners and resistance fighters forming a Lodge in a Nazi prison camp. Loge Liberté Chérie (Cherished or Beloved Liberty Lodge) was established in November 1943; it Initiated, Passed and Raised a single Candidate.

The Lodge met around a table in Hut 6 in the camp Emslandlager VII (Saxony: Germany) which housed some 100 prisoners for 23 hours a day. A Catholic priest provided a Tyler type lookout service. Sadly, only two of the original seven members survived the camp.

Although the Lodge only endured for a few months, its formation testifies to the robustness of the Masonic spirt in the face of unimaginable oppression.

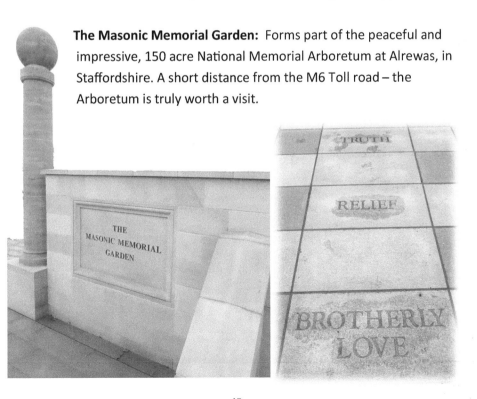

**The Masonic Memorial Garden:** Forms part of the peaceful and impressive, 150 acre National Memorial Arboretum at Alrewas, in Staffordshire. A short distance from the M6 Toll road – the Arboretum is truly worth a visit.

# How is Craft Freemasonry Organised in GB and Ireland?

Craft Freemasonry is organised on three different tiers or levels:

Nationally:        **Grand Lodges**

Regionally:        **Metropolitan Grand Lodges**
                   and/or **Provincial Grand Lodges**

Locally:           **Individual Craft Lodges**

The schematic below shows both the year of establishment of the relevant national Grand Lodges and the numbers of their domestic and overseas Provinces, Groups etc. as at early 2020:

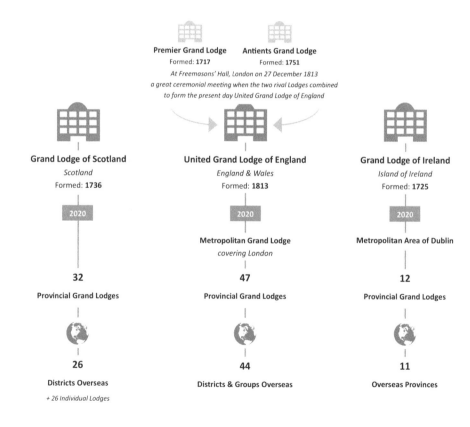

**Premier Grand Lodge**
Formed: **1717**

**Antients Grand Lodge**
Formed: **1751**

*At Freemasons' Hall, London on 27 December 1813*
*a great ceremonial meeting when the two rival Lodges combined*
*to form the present day United Grand Lodge of England*

**Grand Lodge of Scotland**
*Scotland*
Formed: **1736**

2020

**32**
**Provincial Grand Lodges**

**26**
**Districts Overseas**
*+ 26 Individual Lodges*

**United Grand Lodge of England**
*England & Wales*
Formed: **1813**

2020

**Metropolitan Grand Lodge**
*covering London*

**47**
**Provincial Grand Lodges**

**44**
**Districts & Groups Overseas**

**Grand Lodge of Ireland**
*Island of Ireland*
Formed: **1725**

2020

**Metropolitan Area of Dublin**

**12**
**Provincial Grand Lodges**

**11**
**Overseas Provinces**

## United Grand Lodge of England [UGLE]

Not only was the 250th Anniversary of Grand Lodge celebrated at the Royal Albert Hall on 14th June 1967, but so was the Installation of HRH The Duke of Kent as Grand Master of the United Grand Lodge of England; duly annually re-elected to that office to this day. The Grand Master, as a 'Prince of the Royal Blood' has entitlement to appoint a Pro Grand Master to oversee the day-to-day administration and governance of Freemasonry which is the present case.

United Grand Lodge meets four times a year in Quarterly Communication [QC] on the second Wednesdays of March, June, September and December; the appointment/reappointment of the Grand Master is proposed at the December QC and voted upon in the March QC. A Grand Festival Meeting is held on the first Wednesday following St George's Day when it is customary to Install the Grand Master who then appoints the Grand Officers.

**Note:** *See pages 10-11 of the 2019 edition of the Book of Constitutions for a list of Grand Offices*.

At the time of writing (June, 2020) UGLE exercised jurisdiction over 6,566 Craft Lodges in England and Wales, with Metropolitan Grand Lodge accounting for 1,252 (19%) of that total. The number of Lodges in Masonic Provinces varies considerably – here are the smallest and largest six as at the same date:

| Smallest: | | Largest: | |
|---|---|---|---|
| Guernsey & Alderney | 11 | West Lancashire | 342 |
| Jersey | 11 | Essex | 307 |
| Herefordshire | 15 | Hampshire & Isle of Wight | 255 |
| Isle of Man | 19 | Surrey | 253 |
| West Wales | 27 | East Lancashire | 198 |
| Monmouthshire | 29 | Yorkshire – West Riding | 198 |

As the above readily demonstrates, there are considerable variations in Provincial management and administrative demands. In the larger Provinces the Provincial Grand Master might appoint one or more Assistant Provincial Grand Masters to help ensure the smooth running of the Province.

## The Three Risings prior to Closing the Lodge

The Lodge Closing is preceded by the Three Risings. The WM rises and says, 'I rise for the first time' etc. a procedure repeated for a second and third time. The First Rising is to receive communications from Grand Lodge; Second Rising to receive communications from the relevant Provincial or Metropolitan Grand Lodge and finally matters pertaining to our own Lodge under the Third Rising. These Masonic business matters are usually dealt with by the Lodge Secretary – the widespread usage of circulating documents via e-mail has resulted in the conservation of much Lodge time. All Craft Lodge Secretaries receive copies of the business papers and reports arising from Grand Lodge Quarterly Communications – advising their receipt under the First Rising.

## Metropolitan & Provincial Grand Lodges

These provide a delegated administrative service for their respective geographies, in accordance with *the Book of Constitutions*. There is one formal meeting each year, the Annual Communication, during which Officers for the ensuing year (Active Rank) are appointed and other promotions conferred (Past Rank). As an example, a Brother appointed as the current serving Provincial Senior Grand Deacon would be designated as 'PrSGD', but at the end of that year, following the appointment of a successor and assuming no higher promotion was conferred, would hold the rank of Past Provincial Senior Grand Deacon designated as 'PPrSGD'.

**Note:** *Prior to 1971, UGLE administered all of London's Craft Lodges located within a 10 mile radius of Charing Cross. In 1971, the radius was reduced to 5 miles in response to a burgeoning population. Lodges falling within the 5 to 10 mile radial band chose between remaining within the orbit of UGLE, or their relevant geographical Provincial Grand Lodge.* Metropolitan Grand Lodge (MetGL) was formed on 1 October 2003, serve as the administrative authority for London based Lodges.

**Note:** *See page 28 of the 2019 edition of the* Book of Constitutions *for a list of Senior Metropolitan Grand Rank Offices and page 34 for a list of Provincial Grand Offices.*

## Craft Lodge Ranks

It takes a while to get to grips with Masonic ranks — these are the basics:

Everyone starts Masonic life as an Entered Apprentice Freemason (designated as 'EA') progressing to the Second Degree to be Passed as a Fellow Craft (FC) and finally to the Third Degree to be Raised to the Sublime Degree of a Master Mason (MM). EA, FC and MM are all Masonic Ranks.

The next Masonic designation (not a rank) is that of Past Master (PM) accorded to those who have served their Lodge as Worshipful Master. It is considered to be the highest of honours and is only secured through hard work and perseverance. Working our way through what are called the 'Progressive Offices' is the conventional route to what is affectionately referred to as 'the Chair' – these Offices (not ranks) in sequential order *are* Inner Guard, Junior Deacon, Senior Deacon, Junior Warden, Senior Warden. Even so, the Brethren elect a Worshipful Master annually from those who have served as Warden of the Lodge for a year or longer. The convention of rotating through the Progressive Offices is generally faithfully followed. Other long serving Officers such as the Lodge Secretary, aspiring to serve as WM for the first time, may be spared the need to work their way through all the Progressive Offices, other than that of one of the Warden offices.

**Metropolitan and Provincial Craft Honours**

Promotion to Metropolitan or Provincial Office (either Active or Past) is a recognition of Masonic industry – such as having served a Lodge well as its Worshipful Master and continuing to support the Craft thereafter. It is possible to receive Metropolitan or Provincial Craft honours without having first served as a WM based on merit and commitment. For example, a long serving Lodge Secretary might well be considered for honorific recognition.

**How to Differentiate Between English Craft Lodge, Provincial/Metropolitan and Grand Lodge Officers**

This guidance is very much in in the spirit of trying to simplify something that, on first sight, appears to be quite complex:

**Point 1**   Any Brother wearing a pale blue (Cambridge blue) bordered apron will be a Master Mason.

**Point 2**   The substitution of each of the three rosettes with a Level (also called a Tau) on a Master Mason's apron denotes that the Brother has served as a Worshipful Master or is currently doing so.

**Point 3**   Any Brother wearing a Dark Blue or Burgundy (for Stewards) bordered apron is either a Metropolitan/Provincial Grand Officer or a Grand Lodge Officer.

**Point 4**    The maximum width of the coloured border on a Metropolitan or Provincial Grand Lodge Officer's apron is 2 inches; for a Grand Lodge Officer the maximum is 3.5 inches – the former is about thumb length and the latter middle finger length. This is the simplest distinguishing identification method.

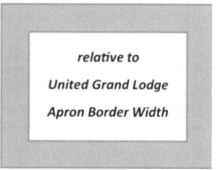

**Point 5**    Burgundy coloured aprons are worn by Stewards holding Provincial, Metropolitan or Grand Lodge Rank; again, Grand Lodge Stewards' apron colour borders are of the wider maximum width of 3.5 inches.

**Point 6**    A Provincial or Metropolitan Grand Lodge Apron displaying three rosettes indicates the promotion of a Master Mason who has not served as WM of a Lodge.

**Point 7**    Metropolitan/Provincial Grand Officer and Grand Lodge Officer uniforms come in two forms – 'Dress' and 'Undress' the former being a more ornate version of the latter and generally only worn on official occasions.

**Point 8**    Rather like the military, the more finesse, gold and detail on a Brother's apron, the higher the rank.

**Note:** *One general point is that a Brother holding 'active' Provincial or Metropolitan Office is referred to as being a 'Grand Lodge Officer' during their tenure; 'holders of 'past' rank being simply referred to as 'Grand Officers'.*

**Note:** *The* Book of Constitutions *has a lot of information on Aprons, Chains, Collar Jewels and Gauntlets supplemented by an illustrated appendix which starts on page 151 of the 2019 edition.*

# How is Masonic Charity Organised?

Each year Freemasons in England and Wales make a vital, positive difference to the lives of many thousands of people. Presently, we collectively provide over £20M of Masonic relief to help people to get back on their feet; surmount adversity; overcome educational and relationship challenges; increase lifesaving medical knowledge; support hospices; help keep our air ambulance services flying and much, much more.

We did all that together through the magnificent medium of the Masonic Charitable Foundation [MCF].

Around 60% of MCF relief funding is directed at supporting the distressed families of Freemasons – often as the result of completely unexpected life changing events.

The *c.* 40% balance is distributed as grants to other, generally people centric, charities making the MCF (us!) one of the largest charitable grant giving organisations in England & Wales.

In addition, many of our private Lodges, Metropolitan and Provincial Grand Lodges and other Masonic Orders independently support local charities and appeals. Consequently, the total level of Masonic charitable giving is an unknown, but it truly makes a very powerful and positive social difference.

**Charity Steward:** In Craft Masonry our tremendous collective effort starts in the heart of every Lodge. Our Bro Charity Steward leads the fundraising in the Lodge for the benefit of both Masonic and non-Masonic charities. From one-off donations, regular Gift-Aid contributions, alms collections, festive board and social activities etc. we enable the MCF to generate that amazing £20M p.a. charitable giving – that is nearly £55,000 per day or £38 per second.

Masonic Provinces enter a period of Festival from time-to-time to raise funds for the MCF. The Provincial Grand Master specifies both a target sum to be raised and the period it is to be raised in – nowadays generally a period of five years. We are encouraged to commit to regular giving throughout the Festival period whilst also supporting a variety of fundraising events; the latter are often open to friends and family members. Of course, no Brother gives any more than can be reasonably afforded and no undue pressure to contribute is ever applied.

Another term we might encounter with regards to Masonic charity is 'Relief Chest'. This name harks back to the medieval Guilds who kept a strong box to hold fines and donations for future charitable or member welfare application. A member of the Guild (Box Master) was charged with looking after the strong box to keep its contents safe – present day Charity Stewards, Lodge Almoners and Treasurers do much the same, via a bank and depository accounts. The Relief Chest scheme has proved very popular with Lodges (around 5,000 active accounts) as it provides a centralised, but segregated depository for dedicated charitable funds. It offers time and administrative saving benefits plus the payment of some competitive interest.

To find out more about the Masonic Charitable Foundation visit their (our) website https://mcf.org.uk/

**Lodge Almoner:** As Freemasons, we are very good at keeping secrets, but sometimes we keep the wrong ones! The shock and rigours of being catapulted into unexpected financial distress, sudden onset of deteriorating health, loss of a loved one etc, are things we innately tend to keep to ourselves. Yet the welfare of its members sits at the very heart of Freemasonry, forming both the rationale for, and remit of, the Lodge Almoner. Brother Almoners maintain regular contact with the sick and distressed members of their Lodges, Lodge widows, the recently bereaved families of a Lodge member, whilst also monitoring the welfare pulse of the wider Lodge membership. Making home and hospital visits; sending cards, flowers and Christmas gifts are all sincerely intended to give people a lift by reminding them that they are in the thoughts of others.

Lodge Almoners also build awareness of the qualifications for, and nature of, the support assistance available from the MCF; assisting Brethren and/or their families to make an MCF relief application. They also liaise with the Provincial or Metropolitan Grand Almoner to help secure the best support outcomes.

The Almoner also has to keep financial receipted records of outgoings – generally the Almoner operates a dedicated bank or Relief Chest account. Christmas usually places a high demand on the Almoner's funds, so Brethren with means often choose to make a personal, festive season 'Alms' donation.

The crucial thing to remember is that the Lodge Almoner should be properly viewed as a 'Confidant' as well as a friend – anything we disclose of a personal nature (provided it is morally sound and lawful) is the Almoner's secret for as long as we wish it to be.

Speak to your Lodge Almoner if you do not have the booklet opposite (or its successor) – should you or your family find that life has unexpectedly catapulted you into a state of distress both the booklet, and the Lodge Almoner, will prove to be good friends.

**Metropolitan/Provincial Grand Lodge Charitable Donations:** Generally, distribute their own charitable funds which are typically topped up annually by both Lodges and individual Lodge members in their orbit. The grassroots collection of donations is usually co-ordinated by Lodge Charity Stewards.

'Matched Funding' schemes are also in common usage, so if an individual Lodge donated £200 to a local good cause the relevant Province might consider adding a further £200. Bro. Charity Steward will know if 'matched funding' is available locally and how to apply for it. An annual event of Provincial Grand Lodge charity giving might also be mounted for the benefit of both Masonic charities and other appropriate local/regional good causes.

**Private Lodge Charitable Donations:** 'Propositions' for charitable donations form an important part of Masonic business proceedings. Each Lodge has its own protocols for charitable giving – Lodge bye-laws sometimes permit a WM, specified Officer or designated group of members to make small charitable disbursements without seeking the formal approval of Lodge members. Otherwise, donations will be formally Proposed by a Lodge Member (who usually gives a brief outline of the charity and donation rationale) and another Brother Seconds the Proposition. The WM then invites the Brethren present at that Regular Meeting to firstly, signify their approval (for) and secondly, to the contrary (against). When we feel moved to propose a small charitable gift, we should make some initial soundings first – a chat with our Bro Charity Steward is a good starting point.

# What are the Basics of Masonic Etiquette?

This term describes the accepted standards of conduct widely employed and respected by Freemasons. We will start with two general points:

1. We should expect it to take some time to become fully acquainted with the Masonic etiquette observed by our own Lodge – expect to make some innocent mistakes along the pathway of learning by experience. We should not feel embarrassed; most Brethren will smile at the remembrance of their own 'early day' mishaps.

2. What follows constitutes basic guidance only – every Lodge tends to finesse the basics, developing local customs and practices, so our regular attendance of Lodge will soon get us up to speed. However, when visiting other Lodges for the first time, expect some variations in protocol; sometimes these can be quite subtle. The virtue of quiet observation comes into its own in our early days as new Masons, but always feel free to ask questions about local etiquette protocols.

**Masonic Etiquette – *Basic Guidance for New and Inexperienced Brethren:***

**Attending Meetings:** We should always read the Lodge Summons – advising our Bro Secretary promptly if we are unable to attend the meeting including any associated Lodges of Instruction and Rehearsal. Similarly, if we are participating in a Ceremony and/or discharging a Lodge Office and cannot attend, we should also advise our Bro Director of Ceremonies as quickly as possible. Even if our attendance may just be in doubt, perhaps we are caring for someone who is unwell who may or may not have recovered before the meeting, we should alert our Bro DC straight away so contingency arrangements can be comfortably put in hand.

**Dress Codes:** Noting the dress code advised on the Summons is strongly advised as this can vary. For example, there may be a request to wear dinner jackets for the annual Installation meeting; some Lodges observe the practice of members wearing black ties in November to mark the month of Remembrance. When visiting other Lodges, the dress code may differ from that observed by our own Lodge, so always ask for a copy of the Summons.

We need to ensure that we are properly dressed before entering the Lodge room – keeping a spare pair of gloves and a black tie in our Masonic cases is a good idea. If we do not need them we may well encounter a Brother in need.

**Late Arrival:** From time to time, our best laid travel plans will be frustrated, and we will be late for a Lodge meeting. Do not panic! If we can safely telephone the Lodge or a fellow attendee to advise that we are running late, that is all well and good. On arrival we should dress and present ourselves to the Tyler who will tell us which Degree the Lodge is in and how far the meeting has progressed. At a suitable juncture, we will be announced and admitted into Lodge taking the Step and showing the Sign of the Degree which is held while we present a short, one sentence explanation for our lateness to the Worshipful Master. Explanation complete, we discharge the Sign and the Bro DC or Bro ADC will escort us to a seat in the Lodge. Getting to Lodge meetings is a bit like a metaphor for life – unexpected and frustrating stuff happens!

**Addressing Brethren during Lodge Meetings:** When in Lodge we are all Brothers. So, if our good friend, Fred Bloggs is holding the Office of Junior Deacon we should not address him as Fred, Bro Fred or Bro Bloggs, but as Bro Junior Deacon. If Fred was a Past Master, Provincial, Metropolitan or a Grand Lodge Officer we continue to address him as Bro Junior Deacon and not Worshipful Brother Junior Deacon. We address the Worshipful Master as just that 'Worshipful Master', not 'WM'. All other Lodge members who are not holding office are addressed as either Brother [surname] or for those who are Past Masters, Worshipful Brother [surname]. If two Brethren share the same surname, then also add the appropriate forename to avoid confusion.

There are other prefixes for higher ranking Grand Officers:

| | |
|---|---|
| *Most Worshipful* (MW) | Grand Master and Pro Grand Master (Present and Past) |
| *Right Worshipful* (RW) | Metropolitan and Provincial Grand Masters (Present and Past) |
| Very Worshipful (VW) | This prefix is applied to certain Grand Lodge ranks (Present & Past) including Grand Chaplains; Grand Registrars; Grand Secretaries, Grand Chancellors; Grand Directors of Ceremonies, Grand Sword Bearers; Grand Superintendents of Works and Grand Inspectors |

**Note:** *The above does not constitute a complete list of rank prefix entitlement which can be found on page 6 of the* Book of Constitutions – 2019 edition.

**Speaking in Lodge:** Emergencies excepted, we never speak out or intervene during a meeting unless we hold an office or are formally presenting Masonic Ritual. If a Brother makes a Ritual error or freezes, we do not articulate a prompt unless specifically tasked to do so. As a visitor we should never try and correct a perceived Ritual error – it is not our job to do so and it might even be a Local Working Ritual variation, so is correct for that particular Lodge.

If we wish to say something in Lodge, then we should speak to our WM and/or Bro Secretary, ideally well in advance of the meeting – they will advise us on both suitability and protocol.

If the WM addresses us in Open Lodge we should rise, take the Step and give the Sign for the relevant Degree and always respond directly to the WM, starting with the words, 'Worshipful Master, …'. The Sign should be held if we are making a short response but discharged if we are being asked to make a report on a Lodge matter. Report complete, and there being no follow up questions from the WM, Step, Sign and sit down. As a general principle, reports should be concise and business like. In some Lodges a Court Bow is preferred in some situations as a courteous acknowledgement of a command or instruction. This is no more than a simple bow of the head.

Masonic Ceremonies and other proceedings are often punctuated by short lulls in activity. Brethren naturally incline to chatting with a neighbour during such lulls which is fine provided such conversations are conducted quietly and discreetly. New and/or inexperienced members should ideally sit with a more experienced Brother who can answer questions or explain proceedings during any suitable lull. Otherwise silence should always be maintained throughout any Ceremony or other Lodge Business matters and conversation ceased immediately on hearing a gavel or Tyler's knocks.  Similarly, during Festive Boards the sounding of a gavel = silence.

**Wine Takings and Masonic Toasts:** As a newmade Brother we all received and replied to the Initiates' Toast during the Festive Board following our Ceremony of Initiation. In early Masonic life the array of 'Wine Takings' and formal 'Masonic Toasts' can seem bewildering.

**Wine Takings:** Are a form of acknowledgement. Customarily, Wine Takings commence with the WM taking wine with the Wardens – subsequent invitations to take wine are entirely discretionary. A high ranking Officer such as the Provincial or Metropolitan Grand Master or their official representative; Grand Officers; Provincial Officers; Brethren who participated in the

Ceremony; a Brother in receipt of a Masonic Promotion or Award; Masters of other Lodges are all typical reasons for being invited to take wine with the WM. The WM might even take wine with everyone present, usually standing whilst the rest of the assembly are requested to remain seated.

When invited to take wine with the WM we simply rise to our feet (unless instructed otherwise) hold our glass aloft before taking a sip and then deferentially nod our head (court bow) to the WM regaining our seat a few seconds later. Our toasting glass can have any liquid in it from water to wine to whiskey. We all need to be mindful of the drink driving laws!

**Formal Masonic Toasts**: Are many and varied although not all are obligatory. Expect to always toast our Monarch (the Loyal Toast) customarily preceded by singing the first verse of the National Anthem. The following is a specimen English Craft Toast list – expect some local/regional variations:

 

**℉ Loyal Toast:** Queen and the Craft

**℉ The Most Worshipful Grand Master**
Currently, His Royal Highness The Duke of Kent

**℉ The Most Worshipful Pro Grand Master** – [Name]
The Right Worshipful Deputy Grand Master   [Name]
The Right Worshipful Assistant Grand Master – [Name]
and the rest of the Grand Officers Present and Past

**℉ The Provincial** or **Metropolitan Grand Master** – [Name]

**℉ The Deputy Provincial** or **Metropolitan Grand Master** – [Name]
**The Assistant Provincial** or **Metropolitan Grand Master(s)** – [Name(s)]
and the rest of the Provincial/Metropolitan/District Grand Officers Present and Past

**℉ The Worshipful Master**

**℉ The Initiate**
only following a Ceremony of Initiation

**℉ The Installing Master**
only following a Ceremony of Installation

**℉ Visitors' Toast**

**℉ Tyler's Toast**

If present, the Provincial or Metropolitan Grand Master will most likely reply to their toast. Conventionally, the Senior Warden proposes a toast to the WM who then makes a reply; similarly, the Junior Warden customarily proposes a toast to visiting Brethren with a nominated visitor replying on behalf of all visitors. Some Lodges and/or Junior Wardens delegate the Visitors' Toast to other Lodge Members, often helping to raise the confidence levels of junior Brethren. There might also be a toast to Absent Brethren; Masonic Charities; Officers of the Lodge; whilst to close the Festive Board we have the Tyler's Toast, usually followed by the Tyler's Song.

Lodges tend to develop their own toasting protocols, so expect to experience some local and regional differences. As examples, some Lodges conclude a toast with Masonic Fire which may or may not include singing – please see 'Masonic Fire' on page 136 for an explanation. In any of the Lancastrian Provinces, expect to hear the Brethren toast the Duke of Lancaster for the Loyal Toast. Henry of Monmouth, Prince of Wales held the title of the 1st Duke of Lancaster from 1386; when he acceded to the throne of England as Henry V in 1413, the title was subsumed into the Crown. Thereafter, the title and the income from the associated Duchy have passed, as a matter of course, to every succeeding monarch, be they Kings or Queens.

**The Internet:** It can be very tempting to conduct Internet searches to find answers to Masonic questions, access Ritual etc. In the early days this might best be avoided for the following reasons:

- We might accidentally discover the details and secrets of a superior Degree spoiling our future experience of that Ceremony.

- There are a number of groups that claim to be Masonic, but are not Warranted by UGLE – these need to be avoided.

- We might happen upon information that comes from an overseas jurisdiction where the Masonic principles are the same, but the Ritual and/or symbolism differ – this can cause some measure of confusion.

- There is a considerable amount of published misinformation on the world wide web about Freemasonry, our Ritual and customs . If we download Ritual from the Internet how do we know it to be correct?

# How should we Make and Respond to a Visitors' Toast?

So, what should we do if called upon to propose or reply to a Visitors' Toast in early Masonic life? If we are unaccustomed to speaking in public, it is best to keep things simple, but structured:

**Proposing a Visitor's Toast:** Our objective is to sincerely acknowledge and thank our Brother visitors for their support, aiming to put a smile on their faces, so creating the desire to visit again. Before the Festive Board we should consult the 'Tyler's Book' which has a separate section where Visitors sign in – this will tell us how many visitors there are in attendance, their Masonic Ranks, Lodge names/numbers and which member of our Lodge is formally hosting them.

If there's a relatively small number of visitors make a note of their names and Lodges. This will enable us to welcome and thank them individually, *"Brethren, this evening we extend a warm Masonic welcome to six visiting Brethren from four Lodges namely, [name them and their Lodges]...".*

If one or more has travelled a considerable distance or comes from a neighbouring Province point this out. If the number of visitors is small, we can emphasise what a big difference their presence has made to the meeting. Also, we can check with those Lodge members hosting a visitor to discover if there is anything noteworthy that we might call attention to – perhaps a Brother has recently been promoted, received an award, celebrated a special occasion or has been appointed to a Lodge Office.

Mentioning the labours (if known) of the next meeting might also encourage return visits. For example, a Ceremony of Initiation would be of interest to recently Initiated Brethren, so we might ask that Brother visitors help spread the word to other local Lodges. Finally, the one thing to avoid at all costs is to comment positively on the Ceremony – this will come across as being self-congratulatory and Masonically inappropriate – we would also be stealing the thunder of the Brother visitor charged with replying to our toast. If not already announced by our Bro. DC, we should say who will be replying to our toast.

Recording some key point notes on a card will help keep our toast on track. If we start to feel breathless or nervous during the toast slow down the spoken delivery of the toast a bit – doing so  sends a calming, 'all is well' message to our brains. Genuinely smiling will have a similar effect.

The following Masonic poem (author unknown) perfectly conveys the spirit of the Visitors' Toast:

*Tonight, I have the pleasure*
*To all I must confess*
*To give to you this toast*
*To our Visitors and our Guests*

*The fellowship that you bring tonight*
*Is something that can't compare*
*You know we like to see you*
*And glad that you're always there*

*The harmony, the chat and jokes we have...*
*With our old and newfound friends*
*We wish it could last for hours*
*And somehow never end.*

*But... all good things must come to an end*
*And we go our separate way*
*We hope you enjoyed yourself tonight*
*And return again someday*

*And now I ask the members to stand*
*To raise a glass in cheer*
*To toast to all our visitors*
*Who supported us this year*
*Our Brother Visitors!*

If we get really stuck we for something to say can always read this poem out (having rehearsed it several times) or seek the creative input of an experienced Brother, such as our Proposer or Bro Mentor etc.

**Replying to a Visitors' Toast:** We may have already discovered that there are a number of Brethren highly skilled at replying to Visitors' Toast – those natural humourists cum raconteurs who seem to hold a Masonic audience almost effortlessly. The chances are that we are probably not that Brother (well, at least not quite just yet) for we lack experience, depth of knowledge etc. Again, having a simple, planned structure will help us to make a good first impression.

Our primary objective is to thank the hosting Brethren for their evening's labours; the welcome and hospitality they warmly extended to us as visitors. We should not forget that we are replying on behalf of all the visiting Brethren. During the meeting make some short notes about the Ceremony and/or other labours/reports and those Lodge Officers/Brethren who actively participated. Congratulate all those Officers who distinguished themselves and the Brother who was Initiated, Passed or Raised.

Do not lose sight of Junior Brethren holding offices such as the Inner Guard or Junior Deacon. A few kind words of sincere encouragement will prove to be highly motivational; our attention to this point will also appreciated by the more experienced Brethren. Did we learn or experience something new during the meeting, or did something strike a chord? If so, we can appreciatively acknowledge that without going into too much detail. A good way of closing is to confirm that we and all the other Brother visitors look forward to visiting again. The important keys are to take a positive approach; to be sincere; be mindful of the hour – Brethren will value our keeping the response brief, as some may have a long journey ahead of them and/or work the following day.

**Masonic Etiquette and Toasting Summary:** This and the previous question have outlined the basic principles of Masonic Etiquette, Wine Taking and Masonic Toasts – every Lodge develops its own protocols and we need to allow ourselves some time to become familiar with them. When visiting other Lodges, the best advice is 'When in Rome, do as the Romans do'. A typical variation might be the timing of salutes during Lodge Openings and Closings – we should honour our host Lodge by following their protocols and procedures.

Rather like Masonic teachings, Masonic etiquette is a process of gradual revelation and memory acquisition gained through direct experience; in the early stages of Masonic life it pays to have our wits about us. Always feel free to ask questions about local etiquette protocols – it will be seen as a mark of genuine interest and sincere respect.

# How did Lodge Room Furnishings Evolve?

**Introduction:** We need to bear in mind that the present day Craft Lodge Room layout and its furnishings, its allegorical and symbolic references, have all evolved over time. The best way to illustrate these points is by example:

Our Lodge rooms are intended to represent the interior of a 'nearing completion' King Solomon's Temple, but our knowledge of the Temple's appearance is incomplete, so certain aspects have creatively evolved to serve the philosophical teachings of Speculative Freemasonry. One example of such a development is the tessellated black

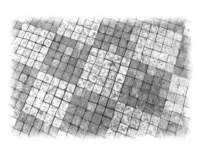

and white pavement. Some illustrated 15th century bibles depicted KST with Masonic style light and dark square flooring. Samuel Lee's extensive illustrations of KST in *Orbis Miraculum (published London 1659)* similarly depicted both the temple's exterior and interior. This style of flooring also featured in many of Europe's grandest buildings and appears to have been adopted by those who created our present day Ritual as the obvious choice for a Lodge room floor covering.

Junior Warden's
Column

Senior Warden's
Column

Similarly, certain features did not exist at the time KST was constructed – such as the celestial and terrestrial maps adorning the globes on the Wardens' columns. Representations of these two columns in English Craft Lodges are now usually situated on the Wardens' pedestals – each column is crowned with a globe – one bearing a celestial map (SW) and the other terrestrial (JW). The column on the Junior Warden's pedestal represents that column explained to us during our Ceremony of Initiation. When KST was built the world was thought to be flat – there were no global maps. Some Masonic scholars consider that bowls for the burning of incense actually crowned the two pillars.

In summary, our Lodge Rooms have developed from the medieval operative workshops replete with tools and stonework in various stages of refinement, including a Perfect Ashlar for Masons to try (check) the integrity of their wooden squares. Early Speculative Masonic meetings were held in private rooms with dining tables, chairs, an open copy of the bible, square and compasses with all the necessary markings chalked on the floor – sometimes the Tracing Board symbols were depicted on a floor cloth that could be simply rolled up and taken away at the meeting's end.

Meetings were conducted with the Brethren seated around a table with toasts being taken throughout. The Lodge 'Called Off' to move from labour to refreshment in order to dine – no food was consumed during the main meeting, but alcohol was. From the mid-18th century the present day set up started to evolve when, for example, the Wardens' columns are believed to have been introduced as tangible, tabletop furnishings.

The origins of lowering and raising the columns is thought to have stemmed from indicating whether the Lodge was 'Called On' to conduct Masonic labour including the taking of toasts or Called Off to dine. Senior Wardens being responsible for the labour part of meetings raised their column to indicate this status; with Junior Wardens sympathetically lowering their columns. The procedure was simply reversed when Calling Off – the Junior Warden being responsible for the dining arrangements.

Tracing boards evolved as a means of explaining Masonic symbols; these had grown considerably in number by the mid-18th century. As previously mentioned, these were either chalked or charcoaled onto the floor or depicted on floor cloths; when the meeting closed the former was wiped away and the latter was simply rolled up for removal. Rooms were hired, so any furnishings had to be easily transported.

The industrial revolution heralded the building and collective ownership of dedicated Masonic Halls in major towns and cities. This inspired the creative development of larger scale and more ornate Lodge furnishings such as Tracing Boards and their draft cabinet housings, carpets, pedestals etc.

Although most Lodges nowadays have a bespoke Lodge Banner there has never been a Constitutional requirement to do so. The tradition stems from a time when Masons often paraded in public, for example, to attend a civic ceremony, such as the dedication of a public building. Historically, banners were employed as a proclamation of identity with members or supporters 'ranging behind' them.

# What are the Progressive Offices in the Lodge?

*There are six progressive offices culminating in the office of Worshipful Master:*

**Worshipful Master and the Senior and Junior Wardens**

These are the three Principal Officers of the Lodge each sitting behind a pedestal on a raised dais of varying heights, the WM's being the highest, followed by the Senior, then Junior Warden. These elevated, historically defensive positions allow the Officers a clear view of the whole Lodge, with the WM, the Principal Officer, conventionally seated farthest from the Lodge entrance. Not always so nowadays with the advent of fire regulations.

On the WM's pedestal we have a closed copy of the Volume of the Sacred Law. The VSL is only opened when the Lodge is Opened in the First Degree with the Square and Compasses placed upon it in a certain position. The WM's collar jewel is the Square. Just a reminder that VSL, Square and Compasses comprise the three Great Lights in Freemasonry.

In close proximity to the WM are a column of Ionic architectural design and a candlestick holding a real or faux candle – these two elements are sometimes combined to form a single furnishing. Both Wardens also have a candle stick and a column, so we have three columns in total, each of different architectural design with a dedicated symbolic meaning. For ease of reference these and other representations are summarised in the table below:

|  | WM | SW | JW |
|---|---|---|---|
| Representing: | King Solomon | Hiram, King of Tyre | Hiram Abiff |
| Column Architecture: | Ionic | Doric | Corinthian |
| Symbolising: | Wisdom | Strength | Beauty |
| Collar Jewel: | Square | Level | Plumb Rule |
| Symbolising: | Moral Rectitude | Equality | Uprightness |
| Lesser Lights: | Master of the Lodge | Sun | Moon |
| Compass Point: | East | West | South |
| Time of day: | Sunrise | Sunset | Meridian (Noon) |
| Spiritual Symbolisation: | Spirit | Soul | Body |

Here is a quote from the Explanation of the First Degree Tracing Board:

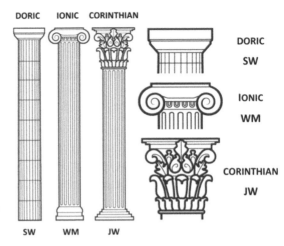

*Our Lodges are supported by three great pillars. They are called Wisdom, Strength and Beauty. Wisdom to contrive, Strength to support, and Beauty to adorn, but as we have no noble orders in architecture known by the names of Wisdom, Strength and Beauty, we refer them to the three most celebrated, which are, the Ionic, Doric and Corinthian.*

The same explanation also informs us that the Master and Wardens each symbolically represent one of the three principal characters concerned with the construction of KST. The WM represents the Wisdom of King Solomon; the Senior Warden the Strength of Hiram, King of Tyre who provided workmen and materials and the Junior Warden, Hiram Abiff, who expressed great Beauty through the mesmerising medium of architectural design.

**The Senior Warden's Place and Duties:**

Placed in the West the SW's duty is, 'To mark the setting sun, to close the Lodge by the WM's command after seeing that every Brother has had his due.' The 'due' referred to would have been the Brethren's daily wage. The Ancient Charges for Operative Masons forbade the practice of working after dark.

The SW's collar jewel is the Level symbolising 'Equality' and the shared responsibility with the WM for the well ruling and governance of the Lodge. The SW also has a gavel to assist the WM in preserving order in the Lodge; places the SW's column in an upright position when the Lodge is Opened to indicate to the Brethren that the Lodge is engaged in Masonic business.

**The Junior Warden's Place and Duties:**

Placed in the South, the JW's duty is, 'To mark the sun at its meridian, to call the Brethren from labour to refreshment and refreshment to labour, that profit and pleasure may be the result.' We have already covered the point that medieval Masons took regular breaks including a 30 minute afternoon nap at the height of summer. The Lodge Foreman would have been responsible for Calling On and Calling Off the Brethren's breaks.

The JW's collar jewel is the Plumb Rule emblemising 'Uprightness', pointing out the responsibility also shared with the WM in the well ruling and governance of the Lodge. The JW also has a gavel to assist the WM in preserving order in the Lodge; places the JW's column in an upright position when the Lodge is Closed, indicating to the Brethren that the Lodge is no longer engaged in Masonic business. The Junior Warden is conventionally responsible for the Festive Board arrangements (often additionally tasked to arrange special events such as a Ladies Evening). It also falls to the Junior Warden to 'prove' any Masonic visitor who is not well known to any of the Brethren present at the meeting.

**Warden:** The word originates from the Germanic word 'Warder' which entered the Northern French language as 'Wardein' and introduced into the English language in the 13th century and was later refined to 'Warden'. Medieval Guilds were not the only organisations to appoint Masons as Wardens. Those charged with maintaining important medieval stone built infrastructures (e.g. London Bridge) often appointed an experienced Mason as the building's Warden to routinely inspect and advise on essential repairs.

## Senior and Junior Deacons [SD and JD]

**Deacon:** The Old English word 'Deacon' is derived from the Greek 'Diakonos' which simply means 'servant'. The first Masonic reference to the office of Deacon appears in 17th century Scotland – the Deacon (singular) being of a much higher status than present day office holders. Deacons (plural) are recorded as holding office in some private Irish and English Lodges from the second quarter of the 18th century. The titles of 'Master's Deacon' and 'Warden's Deacon' appear to be in use as well as the present day office titles. The largely ceremonial offices of Junior and Senior Deacon were not universally adopted in England and Wales until 1815, shortly after the formation of UGLE in 1813.

## The Senior Deacon's Situation and Duties

Situated at or near to the right of the WM, the SD's duty is 'to bear all messages and commands from the WM to the SW and await the return of the JD'. The Senior Deacon also attends on Candidates (serving as a guide) for the Ceremonies and Passing and Raising.

## The Junior Deacon's Situation and Duties

Situated at the right of the SW, the JD's duty is 'To carry all messages and communications of the WM from the SW to JW, and to see that same are punctually obeyed.' The Junior Deacon similarly attends on Candidates for Initiation.

The two Deacons share a common collar jewel and badge of office, usually a Dove carrying an Olive Branch which also forms the finial on the Deacon's wand. This alludes to Noah's release of a dove which later returned to the Ark carrying an olive leaf, so delivering the message that the flood waters had receded.

Some Lodges adopt the practice of making the SD's wand slightly longer than the JD's as an indication of seniority.

In some of the older Lodges alternative collar jewels are sometimes in use. For example, in the Salopian Lodge of Charity No 117,originally constituted in 1810 as an Antients Lodge, an image of 'Mercury the Winged Messenger' serves as the Deacon's collar jewel. This also underpins the point that there is a wealth of historical diversity just waiting to be experienced by visiting other Lodges.

## Inner Guard

In the early Lodges the most recent Initiate effectively acted as the Inner Guard being armed with a trowel. The trowel's point was used to test a prospective Candidate's skin for a sensory response, part of a sensory assessment to prove 'fitness'. First recorded in the Constitutions of 1815, the office of Inner Guard is a feature of English, Scottish and Irish Freemasonry, but is something of rarity in American Blue Lodges; it usually falls to the Junior Deacon to discharge Inner Guard duties. There are English records of early Inner Guard office holders wearing a Trowel collar jewel. However, the Constitutions of 1819 prescribed the usage of the present day Cross-Swords jewel.

## Inner Guard's Situation and Duties

The Inner Guard is situated within the entrance of the Lodge with the duty 'To admit Masons on proof, receive the Candidates in due form and obey the commands of the JW.' Inner Guard is the first of the five progressive offices leading to the Chair.

## Tyler – sometimes referred to as 'Outer Guard'

Although not a Progressive Office, the situation and duties of the Tyler form part of the Lodge Opening Ritual. In Operative Masonry the 'Tiler' enclosed the building with roof tiles, thatch or other materials, so making it a private space. Another variant is a sort of medieval guard – someone who kept watch over the front door of a tavern or inn. In a Speculative setting, the Tyler (possible variant spelling of Tiler) has the duty of ensuring the Lodge is closed to all but those who are qualified to be present.

The method of appointing a Tyler can either be by election or appointed by an incoming WM. Some Brethren enjoy the office so much that they make their services available to Lodges in which they are not members, sometimes providing service for a small fee, a free meal or simply for the love of the Craft. It is the only Lodge office that can be held by a member of another Lodge.

The situation of the Tyler is outside of the door of the Lodge and their duty, 'Being armed with a drawn sword, to keep off all intruders and cowans to Masonry and to see that the Candidates are properly prepared.'

**Cowans to Masonry:** Historically, a Cowan was a maker of drystone walls who, in an operative sense, was relatively more lowly skilled than a Stone Mason and, as such, not qualified to enter a Mason's Lodge. Considered a Scottish term; the Schaw Statutes of 1598 forbade working with or the hiring of 'cowanis' on a penalty of £20 – a huge sum of money back then. In 1707 the records of Mother Kilwinning Lodge defined a Cowan as a 'Mason without the word'. In a broader, modern Speculative sense, Cowan can be taken to mean anyone who is not a Freemason.

The historical custom is that the Tyler is responsible for setting up and breaking down the Lodge. The unwritten, accepted practice is that all able bodied Brethren roll up their sleeves and help out – especially important if the Lodge needs to be broken down to set up the Festive Board. Providing such a service is a perfect distraction from any hunger pangs.

The Tyler's collar jewel is a Sword.

**Note:** *Collar jewel images can also be found on pages 171-179 of the 2019 edition of the* Book of Constitutions.

### Being armed with a drawn sword...

Some of Freemasonry's ceremonial swords are very special, rare, ornate antiquities – worthy of a closer look, but not too close!

## Who Sits Where in the Lodge?

For larger, colour versions of the Lodge layouts below please refer to the Grand Lodge layout plan on the inside front cover of this book – or the alternative Lodge layout on the inside back cover. We will also explore those Lodge Offices not already discussed using the Grand Lodge layout.

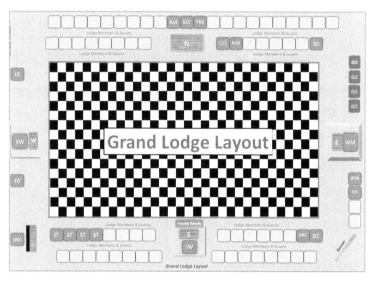

*Grand Lodge Layout*

*Alternative Lodge Layout*

We will start in front of the WM's pedestal and perambulate clockwise around the Lodge. Customarily, there are two fairly grand chairs; one either side of the WM's chair, which we already know represents the 'Throne of King Solomon'.

The seat on the left is usually occupied by the highest ranking Officer present, if not the Metropolitan or Provincial Grand Master it may well be their official representative – most likely a Grand Officer. Other Grand Officers will be seated to the left of the WM in the East.

Before us sits the **Worshipful Master** who, having been duly elected by the Brethren, rules the Lodge for a period of 12 months and wears a collar jewel in the form of a Square. The Charge from the NE encourages us to 'raise a superstructure, perfect in all its parts and honourable to the builder', starting with the foundation stone of Masonic knowledge laid at our Initiation. Many Brethren consider a Brother completes the raising of that superstructure at the end of their first term as WM. The Rough Ashlar of inexperience was transformed into a 'ready to build with' Perfect Ashlar when we are Raised to the Third Degree. The continuing 'building' effort results in the accumulation of a wealth of Masonic knowledge and experience.

To the right of the WM is the **Immediate Past Master** [IPM] – this is not a Lodge Office, but rather a position of rightful recognition earnt through serving the Lodge as WM in the immediate prior term. This is reflected in the IPM's collar jewel – the Square and the diagram of the 47th Proposition of the 1st Book of Euclid suspended within its apex. The 47th proposition (3-4-5 ratio) is the root of all geometry, employed by those ancient skilled Operative builders. In a Speculative setting it recognises that the IPM has successfully applied the philosophical science of Masonry in building a well-founded Masonic life (superstructure). It is incumbent upon every IPM to assist and guide their successors to complete their own superstructures. In practice, the IPM often acts as the WM's Ritual prompter and reassumes the Chair (then generally referred to as a 'Master in the Chair', rather than 'Worshipful Master') if the WM is unavoidably indisposed.

Below is a Past Master's Jewel in heavy gauge Sterling silver hallmarked for 1911, the Square depicting the Sun, Moon and seven Stars.

**Note:** *In Scotland the IPM's Jewel comprises the Square, the Compasses and an Arc; in Ireland it is the Square and Compasses with the capital **'G'** in the centre (G for the Great Architect of the Universe; some Freemasons take to it to represent Geometry)*

**The Chaplain** is seated to the immediate right of the IPM and leads the Lodge in prayers during the Opening and Closing the Lodge; Ceremonies (if deputed by the WM) and says grace /returns thanks at the Festive Board. As Masonic prayers are interdenominational by default, the Chaplain does not have to be an ordained minister of religion. In practice, if such a minister (of any faith) holds Lodge membership they are customarily appointed to the office. During the medieval period, just about everything started and ended with a prayer – for example, the Regius Poem. The Chaplain's collar jewel is a Book in a Triangle mounted on a Blazing Star – in Masonry also called a 'Glory'.

**Note:** *The Chaplain's collar jewel depicted above belongs to the Salopian Lodge of Charity No. 117 – Constituted in 1810.*

Now in the SE corner, immediately adjacent to us is the **Director of Ceremonies** (DC) seated next to the **Assistant Director of Ceremonies** [ADC] – each with a wand held upright in its holder.

Their enjoined duties are to ensure that the Masonic Ceremonies and the constituent Ritual are properly conducted and presented (if necessary, holding rehearsals of the same); ensuring all Brethren are correctly seated according to Office and Rank.

In many Lodges the DC and ADC also act as Ritual prompters; conduct late arrivals to their seat in the Lodge; form up processions both entering into and retiring from the Lodge and actively assist in the Ceremony of Installation. The office of DC is highly demanding, particularly in respect of Masonic Ritual and Procedural knowledge. If we are appointed to an Office, we should always attend any relevant rehearsals and call immediate attention to anything that might frustrate our ability to fulfil our appointed Office.

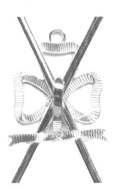

The DC's collar jewel and wand finial is Two Rods in Saltire form tied with a Ribbon – the ADC is the same except the ribbon is substituted with a bar bearing the word 'Assistant'.

**Stewards:** We now perambulate down the south side of the Lodge passing the JW's pedestal to reach the seating area for the Stewards of the Lodge. The WM is free to appoint as many Stewards (subject to availability) as are deemed necessary to meet the needs of the Lodge and its visitors. Duties generally include assisting with the smooth running of the Festive Board, welcoming visiting Brethren and performing small tasks that collectively help to make the Lodge tick. As examples, for a well-attended meeting Stewards might be asked to assist the Deacons with the collection of alms; helping out with charitable fund raising initiatives or as an understudy for a Junior Office (e.g. IG, JD or SD). Whilst this is a logical starting out point for new Brethren to contribute towards the well running of their Lodges, the Office of Steward also calls to older, experienced Brethren. Many a Brother finds a comfortable niche

as a long serving Steward and Masonic Rank is no barrier either – the principle of 'making ourselves more extensively serviceable to our fellow creatures', applies both inside and outside the Lodge environs. Where a number of Stewards are appointed, one might be designated as the Senior Steward. The Stewards' collar jewel comprises a Cornucopia between the extended legs of a pair of Compasses.

The collar jewel opposite is worn by the Brother appointed to serve as Senior Steward for the Salopian Lodge of Charity No 117, seniority being denoted by the presence of a background 'glory'.

**Note:** *In some Masonic jurisdictions just two Stewards are appointed - The Junior & Senior Steward.*

**Organist:** Now in the SW corner of the Lodge we may well be facing our Bro Organist if our Lodge is blessed with one. Alternatively, some Lodges may have a regular 'guest' organist, or a Brother tasked to operate a digital music system. Lodges can only appoint the office of Organist from their membership. The collar jewel of a Bro Organist is a Lyre (small harp like musical instrument).

During our perambulation in the west we pass Bros JD, SW and IG, before turning right to traverse the north side of the Lodge. Midway down we will encounter a desk with two or three Brethren seated behind it namely, and customarily in order of our approach, Bro Assistant Secretary (if appointed), Bro Secretary and Bro Treasurer. In many ways the Brethren seated at this desk form the administrative engine room of the Lodge.

**Secretary:** This is a demanding, but rewarding role often taken up by a Past Master or a very experienced Brother. The issuance of the Lodge Summons, managing correspondence, collation of statistics for Grand Lodge, advising the WM on Constitutional matters, keeping the Lodge minute book, all adds up to a considerable undertaking. Notwithstanding, many Secretaries, having found their true niche, serve their Lodges for long periods.

The Bro **Assistant Secretary** may well deputise for the Lodge Secretary as an understudy, take on delegated administrative tasks to help lighten the Bro Secretary's load. Every Brother should try and make their Lodge Secretary's life as easy as is possible. The Secretary's collar jewel is Two Quill Pens in Crossed Saltire form, tied with a Ribbon and for Assistant Secretary the same except the Ribbon is substituted with a bar inscribed with the word 'Assistant'.

**Treasurer:** The Lodge Treasurer is not appointed by the WM, but is proposed, seconded and then annually elected by Lodge members. Bro Treasurer keeps the Lodge accounts, receives Members' annual subscription dues, makes payments on behalf of the Lodge, including any dues to Metropolitan or Provincial Grand Lodge, and Grand Lodge in London. The Treasurer publishes annual accounts that have been audited by at least two other Lodge members; the resultant annual report is confirmed and approved by the membership. The Bro Treasurer's collar jewel is a Key – a nod back to the medieval Guilds when a Box Master or similar looked after a locked strong box containing the Guild's valuables and coins (there was

no paper money). Much of this money would be used for welfare and charitable purposes. Today our Lodge Treasurers, Charity Stewards and Almoners work closely together as each has to maintain financial records.

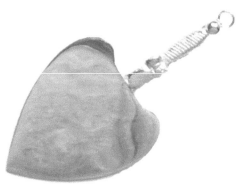

**Charity Steward:** Just past the desk sits the Bro Charity Steward alongside Bro Almoner – the duties of both Officers are described and explored in the 'Organisation of Masonic Charity' question dealt with on pages 51-53.

The Bro Charity Steward's collar jewel is a Trowel.

**Almoner:** During the Ceremony of Installation, Lodge Officers are appointed or reappointed for the ensuing year. In most cases, prescribed Ritual wording summarises the duties of the relevant Offices, but not for the appointment of Lodge Almoner. Quite rightly, it is for every WM to find their own fitting words, tailored to the individual Brother being appointed, to describe the fulfilment of such a sensitive welfare role.

Older Brethren may recollect a time when most NHS hospitals had someone in post as Almoner. Their role was to form a communication bridge linking patients awaiting discharge with local social, welfare and healthcare services. Tailored to the needs of each patient, this crucial caring role made a world of difference to those recovering from illness and injury. Both Lodge and hospital Almoners epitomise the great gift of bringing relief to those in distressed and challenging circumstances.

The Lodge Almoner's collar jewel is a Scrip-Bag bearing a Heart upon it.

A Scrip-Bag was a medieval leather pouch often used by pilgrims as an alms purse.

The term derives from the Old English word 'scrippe' which took its rise from the Old French word 'escrepe'.

**Lodge Mentor:** There is no allocated seat or station for the Lodge Mentor, who will most likely be found sitting among new and inexperienced Brethren. Our Bro Mentor's primary aim is to co-ordinate the mentoring activities within the Lodge. These will include ensuring that every new Brother has a personal mentor to help them to find their feet on the Square. Continuing mentoring support is directed at helping each and every Brother find a comfortable level of participation. For some of us, it might be that family and work duties limit our initial involvement; we might wish to work our way towards becoming Master of the Lodge or simply find happiness in a more a supportive role either on the floor of the Lodge or behind the scenes. The crucial point is that none of us should ever feel pressurised into pursuing a particular course. It can take quite some time for each of us to come to a reasoned conclusion about how we wish to engage with Freemasonry. We need to be patient with ourselves as much as those around us do. Even so, attitudes, opportunities and personal circumstances are all capable of changing over time, so nothing should forever be set in stone.

The Lodge Mentor's collar jewel is Two Chisels in Saltire.

**Note:** *Images of the Collar Jewels referred to can be seen on pages **171-179** inclusive of the 2019 edition of the* Book of Constitutions.

**Voluntary Service:** In bringing matters to close, it is important to never lose sight of the point that Freemasonry is a voluntary service organisation. Those Brethren who give their time, energy, enthusiasm and knowledge to fulfilling a Lodge Office do so for no reward, other than personal satisfaction. We all need to keep this at the forefront of our minds and make life as easy as possible for all our active Lodge Officers. Some of the smiles we send out today will surely be returned to us in the times ahead.

**Collar Jewel Image Credits:** Sincere and fraternal thanks to the Salopian Lodge of Charity No 117 for allowing their venerable collar jewels to be photographed and depicted and to 'The Lodge Room (Masonic Regalia) – www.thelodgeroom.co.uk' for providing images of the present day collar jewels. KM

# Why does the Number '3' Feature Prominently in Masonry?

The comprehensive exploration of this question would require its own book, so please consider the following as an introduction:

Throughout history the number '3' has been considered to be both Powerful and Divine. We will start our short exploration in the company of the 6th century BCE Greek philosopher and mathematician, Pythagoras. Born around 570 BCE in Samos, Ionia (now part of Turkey) Pythagoras studied philosophy from a young age. Many of his wisdoms have travelled through the ages, some clearly influencing those free thinkers who established Speculative Freemasonry.

Here are three examples:

1.      No man is free who cannot control himself

2.      Friends are as companions on a journey, who ought to aid each other to persevere in the road to a happier life

3.      Do not say a little in a lot of words but a great deal in a few

Pythagoras and his followers believed that triangles and the number '3' could be used to explain and solve all the mysteries of the universe. Whoever ultimately achieved this feat would themselves become omnipotent. He was by no means the first to think in this way, as the geometrical use of triangles originated from the pyramid building Egyptians. They claimed that their geometrical knowledge was given to them by beings from 'beyond this world' they referred to as 'Gods'. Consequently, many of our world's ancient religions and great philosophers came to consider the triangle to represent 'deity' or 'God' and 'perfection'. Later on in Freemasonry, the equilateral triangle was adopted as the ultimate 'Deity' symbol.

Pythagoras was the first to disseminate this founding 'geometrical' knowledge beyond the borders of Egypt; we have already explored the Regius Poem legend of how Pythagorean geometrical knowledge first came to England during the reign of King Athelstan in the 10th century CE.

As to the wider claim that every mystery can be solved using triangles and the number '3', we each have to draw our own conclusion. Here are some 'Powerful 3s' to contemplate:

- We live on the planet Earth – the third planet closest to the sun.

- In 1966 the mystery of human DNA was unravelled – its code consists of chains of three linked (triplet) Nucleotide molecules called 'Codons'; the essence of life itself is fashioned out three core ingredients DNA, RNA and Proteins; the DNA strands forming a double-helix are actually linked together by a third constituent, namely hydrogen.

- Human perception works in 3s – we perceive two objects, simultaneously recognising that both are separated by the space (third element) between them. Consider the way the we learn to read; our eyes scan each letter separately (as pictures) with the relationship between a pair of letters defined by a small amount of white space. Two letters connected by white space = 3 elements.

- Three forms of memory are involved in adding a new word to our vocabulary – Audio Memory deals with how the word sounds when correctly pronounced; Visual Memory records a picture allowing us to see how the word is spelt whilst our Semantic Memory archives the word's meaning.

- We find it easier to remember information and facts when they are grouped into threes and even more memorable when the classic three phase presentation mantra is employed of, 'Tell them (the audience) what you are going to tell them; tell them' and then 'tell them what you told them'.

For the latter point, this outline, present and summarise format can be readily observed in the structure of all mainstream TV and radio news broadcasts. Also think about the Ceremony of Initiation – how many times did we repeat the 'word' after it had first been entrusted to us?

The creators of Freemasonry clearly recognised the importance of the number '3' both as a Powerful and Divine number.

As a faith based fraternity, we symbolically recognise a right-angled triangle to represent 'Universal Nature' and an equilateral triangle to symbolise the 'Supreme Being' whose all seeing eye observes our words and actions. This implies an extra-terrestrial Divine triangular connection between our Words, Actions and God which was alluded to when we took the Obligation of an EAFM - Bro Deacons held their wands in triangular form above our heads.

Organising Freemasonry's core allegorical moral messages into groups of three made them easier to remember – an application of the 'art of memory'. Weighing these matters up, we may well reach the conclusion that our heavy reliance on the number '3' makes pyramid builders of us all!

In Part 3 of The New Mason's Friend we will tour through the Ceremony of Initiation – those elements grouped in threes are indicated thus, '(3)'.

**Part 2**

# Fast History Timeline

**London Bridge *c.* 1616** – *stone built – Wardens (customarily experienced Operative Masons) were appointed to monitor and advise on maintenance matters.*

81

# 50+ *Fast History* Timeline Events impacting upon Freemasonry

1346-1350      **The first Plague Pandemic** rages through Britain resulting in the population being greatly reduced. It causes unimaginable social, economic and governance shocks – the catalyst for bringing the Feudal system to an end by around 1500. Reeling from the shock, many trades needed to reorganise their governance structures – see below. The human devastation brought all building works and stone quarrying to a halt.

1356-1376      **The London Masons' Company** (Guild) established as Operative Masonry began to recover from the impact of the first plague pandemic – there may well have been other London-based Guild-like masonry institutions before this date, but we do not have any written records.

1425-1450      **Regius Poem** was penned – oldest Masonic document – thought to have been copied from an even older document – chiefly concerned with recording the 'Ancient Charges' or regulations governing Freemasonry reputedly dating from first half of the 10th century.

1492-1498      **Columbus** discovers the New World (1492) and on a third voyage discovers South America (1498).

1500 onwards      **The Feudal system,** which enslaved most of the post Norman conquest peasantry, has effectively ended in England and Wales – largely due to the economic and social impact of the plague – most peasants are now paid a wage to work the land or hold small agricultural tenancies. Ecclesiastical building is in serious decline. Over the next 150 years, Spain imported huge quantities of gold and silver from the New World. Much of the silver is destined for China as it was the country's sole trading currency. Such was the supply of silver, that its rise in value caused inflation to rocket around much of the civilised world – wage earners bore the economic brunt – their waged spending power went into long term decline – they progressively became poorer.

| | |
|---|---|
| 1535 | **The first full English translation of the Old Testament** was published on 4th October 1535. Translated by William Tyndale and Myles Coverdale – Tyndale died before finishing the work which was completed by Coverdale. Prior to this date only Latin Bibles would have been displayed in Lodge meetings. |
| 1536-1540 | **Henry VIII Dissolution of the Monasteries** some 900 economically active monastic estates controlling 25% of the land in England effectively closed making thousands of workers redundant. Masonry loses one of its largest clients, seriously impairing all of the construction related Guilds. |
| 1576 | **The Geneva Bible** both Testaments first published in England from 1575; depicts woodcut illustrations of KST. |
| 1590-1598 | **William Schaw:** King's Mason to James VI of Scotland sets out to reform the organisation of Scottish Freemasonry, resulting in the publication of *The First Schaw Statute* (1597/8) comprising 22 Clauses (Charges) regulating the governance of Masonry in Scotland. These included the stipulation that minutes of all Lodge Meetings be recorded – an administrative first – the earliest Lodge minutes date to 1599. |
| 1603 | **Union of Crowns** followed the death of Elizabeth I, with James VI of Scotland gaining accession to the crowns of England and Ireland – unification = reduced demand for castle, defensive town/city walls and castellated manor house building. |
| 1603 onwards | **New World wealth of merchants** etc. funds the building of many fine stone built halls and grand homes, constructed in the then fashionable European style; their taxes also greatly contribute to the funding of civil infrastructure developments. |
| 1611 | **King James Bible published** |
| 1620-1621 | **London Masons' Company** (Guild) record book records the term 'The Acception' which seems to refer to a group of non-operative Masons attached to the Company. |
| 1634 | **First Speculative Masons Initiated in Scotland** recorded in the minute book of the Lodge of Edinburgh; still in existence today as The Lodge of Edinburgh (Mary's Chapel) No 1. The Lodge minutes date back to 1599. |

| | |
|---|---|
| 1642 | **English Civil War** starts, dividing the country into Loyalists and Parliamentarians – culminated with execution of Charles I for treason on 30th January 1649. |
| 1646 | **Elias Ashmole** made a diary record of his Initiation into the Lodge of Lights in Warrington on 4th October at 4.30pm – the first recorded Initiation of an Accepted English Mason in England – the list of Lodge Members present points to 'Accepted' membership having been established sometime prior to this record date. Scottish Masonry can fairly lay claim to the first recorded Initiations of Accepted Brethren. |
| 1665 | **The Great Plague of London** wreaks havoc. An estimated 100,000 people, around 25% of London's population, die from the plague over an 18 month period. |
| 1666 | **Great Fire of London** destroys the centre of London but helps quell the plague. Most buildings rebuilt with fire resilient brick and roof tiles; Operative masons mainly benefit from the rebuilding of churches. |
| 1682 | **Elias Ashmole** makes a diary record of attending Lodge at Masons' Hall, in London when six persons were admitted into Freemasonry referring to them as 'New-Accepte' Masons. |
| 1685 | **James II** (James VII of Scotland) enthroned as the last Roman Catholic monarch of England, Ireland & Scotland. Deposed during the 'Glorious Revolution' of 1688. Attempted to recover his thrones, but after losing the Battle of the Boyne in 1690 retired to France to live in exile. |
| 1688 | **Jacobite uprisings start**; primary aim is to restore James II (James VII of Scotland) to his thrones – these continue through to 1745 with allegiance switching to James's House of Stuart successors. Jacobite support of two planned French invasions of England in 1744 and 1759 – these plans do not come to fruition. |
| 1694 | **Bank of England established** as the wars waged by William III resulted in significant national debt – the bank was established as the sole issuer of high denomination, promissory paper banknotes. |

| 1695 | **Bank of Scotland established** – the following year, became first European bank to issue paper currency. |
|---|---|
| 1701 | **Act of Settlement** places the House of Hanover as successors to the English throne. |
| 1707 | **Ratification of the Act of Union** between England and Scotland. |
| 1714 | **Queen Anne**, the last Stuart monarch dies on 1 August; George I, the first Hanoverian monarch, accedes to the throne of a unified England and Scotland. This fuels Jacobite geopolitical tensions. |
| 1717 | **The first Grand Lodge** formed in London on 17th June; Anthony Sayer – Gentleman is the first Grand Master of the premier Grand Lodge of England. |
| 1721 | **John Duke of Montagu** elected Grand Master; premier Grand Lodge starts meeting in Quarterly Communication; begins to evolve as Freemasonry's regulatory authority. |
| 1723 | **The Constitutions of Masonry** the premier Grand Lodge of England's rule book for the governance of Freemasonry is published; William Cowper  'Clerk of the Parliaments' is appointed Secretary of the Grand Lodge to record minutes of the quarterly meetings. |
| 1725 | **Grand Lodge of Ireland** established – initially providing Masonic governance over the island of Ireland which continues to this day with the addition of Provinces overseas. |
| 1725-1760s | **Freemasonry arouses considerable public interest;** meetings and ceremonies were advertised in the Press; journalists published papers, pamphlets and articles claiming to reveal Masonic secrets; publicity results in many of the 'good and the great' of the time joining the Craft – Freemasonry became fashionable! |
| 1730 | **Premier Grand Lodge then controlled over 100 Lodges** in England and Wales and had warranted overseas Lodges in Madrid and what was then called Calcutta, which has now reverted to its pre-British administration name of Kolkata. |

| 1730-1765 | **The beginnings of American Freemasonry** start with the formation of the Grand Lodge of Pennsylvania in 1730; Grand Lodges gradually form across the American Colonies culminating with the Grand Lodges of New Jersey 1761 and Delaware 1765. |
|---|---|
| 1733 | **St. John's of Boston** was the first recorded Lodge in America – there are some indications that the first unrecorded Lodge may have dated to *c.* 1720. |
| 1736 | **Grand Lodge of Scotland** established. |
| 1737 | **The Son of George II**, HRH Frederick Lewis, The Prince of Wales was made a Mason, the first Royal member of the Craft. This greatly enhances the social standing of Freemasonry. |
| 1740-1750 | **An influx of Irish Masons into London**. Many claimed great difficulty in gaining admission to the London Lodges and later went on to state that premier Grand Lodge had departed from the 'Ancient Landmarks' prescribed in the rules of Masonry said to have been established in York under the patronage of Prince Edwin in 926. (See 'What is Freemasonry's oldest document?' Part 1: p. 36). |
| 1751 | **London based Irish Masons** form their own Grand Lodge which became known as the Antients Grand Lodge; they referred to members of the longer established premier Grand Lodge as the 'Moderns'. This division endured for 63 years but, over this period it seems that some Brethren held membership of both Grand Lodges. |
| 1754-1763 | **The French and Indian War** was a long running conflict between the American colonies of British America and those of New France. Some troops formed military Lodges under the constitutions of the Moderns, Antients, Scottish and Irish Grand Lodges. The number of Military Lodges was estimated to be around 50. The conflict later coincided with the more global Seven Years' War of 1756-63; from a European perspective the French and Indian War was subsumed into the Seven Years' War; American historians tend to view the two conflicts as being quite separate and distinct. |

| | |
|---|---|
| 1775-1782 | **The American War of Independence** reached its end following the British surrender at Yorktown in 1781, bringing British political support for war to an end. The British Government sought to outmanoeuvre the French nation, its regional arch-rival, by striking a peace time trade deal with the Americans; The Anglo-American Treaty was announced on 30th November 1782 – the treaty effectively marginalised the French who shortly agreed their own peace terms. Some Military Lodge members stayed on and appear to have been helpful in establishing Grand Lodges in the Eastern States. |
| 1787-1799 | **The French Revolution**; a cocktail of social and economic factors led to the Revolution – the Feudal system had been retained in France angering the peasant classes; the bourgeoisie middle class were denied access to political office or honorific recognition; population headcount explosion meets major crop failures; near national bankruptcy due to funding support of the American Civil War; new sources of gold entering the market cause high inflation and a loss of faith in the monarchy. Against this backcloth the need for social reform became the mainstay of intellectual debate in many of the established Societies including Masonic Lodges. |
| 1799 | **The Unlawful Societies Act of 1799** enacted by British parliament in response to the French Revolution being fearful of republicanism reaching the British Isles. The Act attempted to control Trade Union activity by banning meetings of those groups requiring the taking of oaths or obligations as a condition of membership. This almost closed down Freemasonry. However, The Earl of Moira, acting Grand Master of premier Grand Lodge and The Duke of Athol, Grand Master of the Antients Grand Lodge, made joint representation to William Pitt (the Younger) the British Prime Minister at the time. The upshot was conditional permission from Parliament for the continuance of Masonic meetings; the 'condition' was that every Lodge had to make an annual return to their local authority comprising a list of members' names, ages, addresses and occupations. This requirement was not formally rescinded by Parliament until the 1967 Criminal Justice Act was enacted. However, an attempt in |

1939 to have the membership registration requirement repealed resulted in an understanding that the Attorney General would not pursue Private Lodges for non-compliance. This informal accommodation was due to a lack of Parliamentary debating time in the World War II years.

| | |
|---|---|
| 1809 | **The two rival Grand Lodges** appoint Commissioners to negotiate their Union. |
| 1813 | **United Grand Lodge of England founded.** At Freemasons' Hall, London on 27 December a great ceremonial meeting when the two rival Lodges combined to form the present day United Grand Lodge of England (UGLE). The first Grand Master was HRH The Duke of Sussex, the youngest son of King George III. The union ushered in a period of consolidation – the old counties were established as Masonic Provinces. One exception was the establishment of Wales as a single Province (later split into three Provinces). Masonic administration protocols, ranks, regalia etc. all became standardised. |
| 1814 | **647 UGLE administered Lodges in England & Wales** |
| 1815 | **The offices of Inner Guard, Junior and Senior Deacons** universally prescribed for the first time under the English Constitution. Deacons were a pre-unification feature of Antient Lodges and were universally adopted as part of the unification negotiations. Inner Guard dates back somewhat further in time – the most recent Entered Apprentice usually being appointed to the office being armed with a trowel. |
| 1815-1900 | **Britain boomed** feeling the full benefits of the Industrial Revolution; excelling at new technological innovations particularly in the engineering of machines for industrial mass production. The economic benefits were considerably amplified through global trade, particularly with the colonies in North America and the Caribbean and through unrivalled political influence in countries such as India. Industrial led urbanisation drew people from the countryside to work in the rapidly growing towns and cities. The evolution of the railways also boosted economic growth – despite being punctuated by |

occasional periods of downturn, the general economic environment was very positive for this period. Much building of bespoke Masonic Halls took place in major urban centres – many still in service today.

1875      **HRH Albert Edward, Prince of Wales** was elected as Grand Master ushering in a formidable period of growth for Freemasonry. Always in the public eye, the Grand Master often appeared in full regalia to perform public ceremonies such as laying the foundation stones of major public buildings. Such enthusiastic public support ensured that Freemasonry was frequently reported in the local, regional and national newspapers.

1901      **The Prince resigns as Grand Master** to ascend to the throne as King Edward VII – by the end of his tenure the number of UGLE administered Lodges stood at 2,800 – more than quadrupling in number since UGLE's formation some 87 years earlier.

1914-1918      **The Great War, dubbed 'the war to end all wars'.** Some 16 million people, military and civilians, died during the conflict. More than 3,000 English and Welsh Freemasons are known to have died.

1918 -1919      **1918 Influenza Pandemic.** It is estimated that 500 million people worldwide contracted what was rather inaccurately called 'Spanish Flu' resulting in 50M to 100M fatalities. In the UK 228,000 deaths were recorded.

1927-1934      **Freemasons' Hall** was built in Great Queen Street, London on the site where Freemasons have been regularly meeting since 1775. Constructed in magnificent *art deco* style, the building is an enduring memorial to the 3,000+ Freemasons who lost their lives in WW I. Freemasons' Hall; its museum and library are open to the public for free guided tours.

*Note: It is advisable to pre-book such tours, as the building is also a popular events and TV and film set venue – for example, parts of the TV series Spooks and Agatha Christie's Hercule Poirot were filmed there. This means some of the principal areas are not always open, so it is worth checking beforehand.*

| 1939-1945 | **World War II** The deadliest conflict in recorded human history resulted in up to 85M deaths worldwide. In the three years following the end of hostilities, some 650 new Lodges were established in England and Wales largely to accommodate returning servicemen seeking to maintain comradeship in the tranquil and peaceful Masonic environment. |
|---|---|
| 1967 | **250th Anniversary of Grand Lodge** celebrated at the Royal Albert Hall on 14th June, centring on the Installation of HRH The Duke of Kent as Grand Master; duly annually re-elected to that office to this day. |
| 1969 | **The Committee of The Emulation Lodge of Improvement for Master Masons** [ELI] sponsored the publication of their Emulation Ritual book. Emulation Ritual is arguably the most widely used, post-unification form of Masonic Ritual being initially approved by the newly formed United Grand Lodge in June 1816. Thereafter, successive ELI Committees have faithfully preserved Emulation Ritual, except for those changes required, and approved of, by Grand Lodge. |
| 1992 | **275th Anniversary of Grand Lodge.** Celebrated at Earls Court on 10 June with over 12,500 Freemasons and guests in attendance. The event also established a precedent – the first time the print and broadcast media were given access to a Grand Lodge meeting. |
| 2017 | **Tercentenary of Grand Lodge.** Many Masonic celebrations throughout the land, particularly in June. Our Grand Master, HRH The Duke of Kent, presided over the Especial Meeting of Grand Lodge in the Royal Albert Hall on 31 October. The meeting was attended by 136 representatives of sovereign Grand Lodges. A DVD of this event was produced – check if your Lodge has a copy; it should also be available on YouTube. |
| 2020 | **Numbers of Craft Lodges.** At the time of writing UGLE exercised jurisdiction over 6,566 Craft Lodge in England and Wales, with Metropolitan Grand Lodge accounting for 1,252 (19%) of that total. In response to the COVID-19 pandemic Grand Lodge suspends all Lodge Meetings until July 2020. |

# Part 3

# The Ceremony *of* Initiation – Explored

*King Solomon's Temple (not to scale)*

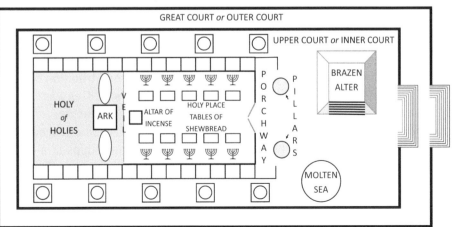

# The Ceremony *of* Initiation - *Emulation Ritual*

Getting to grips with Freemasonry's archaic Ritual, symbolism and distant past can seem rather daunting in the early days of Masonic life. However, help is at hand with a guided tour of the Ceremony of Initiation, accompanied by a comprehensive glossary (Part 5) to help cut through the archaic language. This is supported in Part 4, with a look at Medieval Apprentices and their Masters.

Masonic Ritual can be rather kaleidoscopic as some of the allegorical content can have more than one interpretation. It is simply not possible to cover all the variations in this work and for that reason we should consider the following tour as the author sharing a 'personal interpretation' of the Ceremony of Initiation and not necessarily a consensus perspective. For example, the symbolic spiritual representations of the three Principal Officers (Body, Soul & Spirit) is an interpretation that other Brethren may not have considered. Time and experience allows each us to interpret Masonic Ritual to identify those philosophical values that best work for us.

Before commencing the tour, we will take a quick look at the adoption of Emulation Ritual under the English Constitution and how it was memorised.

## Emulation Ritual

In 1969, the Committee of The Emulation Lodge of Improvement for Master Masons [ELI] sponsored the publication of their Emulation Ritual book. Emulation Ritual is arguably the most widely used, post-unification form of Masonic Ritual. Thereafter, successive ELI Committees have faithfully preserved Emulation Ritual, except for those changes required and approved by Grand Lodge. This does not happen very often – key changes were last made in 1986.

Emulation Ritual was initially memorised in the medieval oral tradition of listening to the words, and then repeatedly articulating them. This was achieved by regularly attending Lodge, including Lodge of Instruction meetings, supplemented by one-on-one instruction from an experienced Mason, typically a Brother's Proposer. However, in this friendships-at-a-distance, digital age, such support may be limited and further constrained by work and family demands. In Part 6 of this book we will explore a scientifically founded method for committing Masonic Ritual to long-term memory.  More about that later.

It is customary to present Brethren with a Ritual Book, covering all Three Degrees, at the time of being Raised to the sublime degree of a Master Mason. Entered Apprentices may like to know that it is possible to purchase a separate Lodge of Emulation Ritual Book for the First Degree. The books also includes the relevant Emulation Lectures – these are in a question and answer format, describing the moral and symbolic significance of the First Degree. Similarly, for those Passed to the Second Degree, there is a separate ELI Ritual and Lectures book. The Lectures need to be considered within an historical context as they date back to 1817 and the language is consequently archaic.

*Our exploratory tour starts overleaf...*

# The Ceremony *of* Initiation – *Emulation Ritual* – Exploration

## Introduction:

 The Ceremony of Initiation is often described as our being 'reborn' to begin a new life as a Freemason. So, we are symbolically reborn unclothed, free of material possessions, uneducated and in a state of helplessness.

Our Masonic experience really started when we first conceived the notion of becoming a Freemason. The germ of that idea then positively developed as our embryonic interest grew through an exchange of information – formal interview, chatting to family, friends, Lodge members etc. – to arrive at that happy point where the Lodge approved our application for membership. Advised of the date for our Initiation we had advance knowledge of our Masonic birthday. However, the Ceremony of Initiation does not stop at the point of rebirth but continues to begin our Masonic education. This educational process needs to continue until we have such a sound grasp of the basic Masonic teachings, symbolism and principles that we are both judged to be, and personally feel, ready for the next step.

Being Passed to the Degree of a Fellow Craft means we are now able to continue our Masonic learning in the Second Degree. This is largely achieved by our own industry, albeit under the watchful eyes and active support of the more experienced Brethren around us.

 Later on, Masonic maturity and a sense of graduation beckon when we are Raised to the sublime degree of a Master Mason (Third Degree). Our attention will then be directed towards helping Brethren in the First and Second Degrees advance their Masonic knowledge. This support can take many forms including presenting Masonic Ritual.

The number '3' regularly features in Craft Freemasonry and is considered to be both a 'Powerful' and a 'Divine' number. Look out for the (3) signposts along the way.

Returning to the Ceremony of Initiation (Emulation Ritual) we will now refresh and hopefully deepen our experience of it seeking to:

- gain a sound appreciation of the integral symbolic teachings
- feel better connected to our medieval Operative past – Part 4
- fully comprehend the archaic language via a glossary – Part 5

To begin with, we will break the Ceremony down into 14 sections:

1. Preparation – before entering the Lodge
2. Admission – into the Lodge
3. Pass before Brethren
4. Advancing to the Pedestal
5. Obligation
6. The moment Masonic life begins – Greater & Lesser Lights
7. Physical Penalties & Entrustment
8. Testing by the Junior & Senior Wardens
9. Apron Investiture
10. Charge in the North-East Corner
11. The Working Tools of an Entered Apprentice Free Mason
12. Explanation of the First Degree Tracing Board
13. The Lodge Warrant
14. Charge after Initiation

## 1]    Preparation - before entering the Lodge

We will probably never forget being ushered into a small room adjoining the Lodge to be prepared for our Initiation by a Brother we now know to be the Tyler. Our nerves already running somewhat on the high side, we were further tested when we were asked to undertake an apparently bizarre range of preparatory measures. Rearranging our clothing to expose some of our skin; new, intriguing neck apparel; alternative footwear, but rather oddly, only for one foot; depositing certain items with the Tyler and finally experiencing a disorientating reduction of sensory capacity. In a state of general bewilderment, we shuffled our way to the Lodge door under the guidance of the Tyler. What on earth was going on?

The Emulation Lectures provide a symbolic insight for some of these preparations, for example, the items the Tyler asked us to deposit. Three (3) reasons are given namely:

1.      We should not bring anything offensive or defensive into the Lodge – this harks back to the times when swords and daggers had to be legally worn in public as a peace keeping measure. There was a social hierarchy of offensive weapons and defensive armour to be carried or worn originally determined in the 13th century by the amount of land owned. However, weaponry was usually surrendered when attending meetings, social functions, church etc.

2.      That we should be received into Lodge in a state of poverty to remind us of the needs of others.

3.      King Solomon forbade the sound of metallic tools at the Temple's construction site – consequently all the building's materials were pre-prepared off site, each piece of stonework given an assembly identification

*Henry VI silver Groat* - 1340/41
*(worth 4 old pennies)*

mark and transported for the ordered 'hushed' construction. We might also note Exodus 20 which details the commandments handed to Moses by God; verse 25 states, 'And if thou wilt make me an altar of stone, thou shalt not build it of hewn stone: for if thou lift up thy tool upon it, thou hast polluted it.' (King James Bible).

We can also add the point that none of us were born with any material possessions, or clothing come to that.

Three explanations are given for our reduced sensory perception:

1.      Not being able to perceive the form of the Lodge just in case we have a last minute change of heart about proceeding with the Ceremony.

2.      A reminder to keep the wider world in the dark with regard to Masonic secrets and mysteries.

3.      That 'our hearts should conceive before our eyes perceive' which implies the formation of a strong emotional commitment to Masonic life, its virtues and demands, sometime prior to our joining the Craft.

Some consider sensory deprivation was a later addition to the Ceremony, possibly following a time of conflict or political uncertainty when some Lodge Members wished to keep their identities hidden before the Candidate's Obligation had been completed. It is also considered to symbolise birth, as all infants are born out of the darkness of the womb into the light of the world.

The footwear explanation given in the Lectures does not chime at all with what is actually being practised; the Lectures refer us to the time of the burning bush, when Moses was instructed by God to remove his shoes before walking on holy ground. The preparation actually experienced does not involve the removal of both shoes. The practice of being 'slip-shod' is more about appearing to be 'poor' and 'worn down at the heel'. There is also an ancient custom of publicly signifying acceptance of a contract by removing a shoe and temporarily passing it to the counterparty – a bit like shaking hands on a deal.

If included in medieval ceremonies, the removal of a shoe may have signified that the Apprentice was prepared to acquiesce to a serious Obligation. Another possibility is that it indicated he was already contracted to his Master sometime before (as long as a year and a day) his formal Initiation.

The Lectures offer no explanation about the adjustment to clothing, but there are various insights as follows:

1. As proof of gender – but is this really a reliable methodology?

2. To bring our skin into contact with the Lodge, particularly whilst kneeling during the Obligation; similarly exposing our heart before the VSL; hand on VSL.

3. At the time Speculative Freemasonry evolved it was not uncommon to secrete a blade up the right sleeve. **Note:** *the left-hand (Latin: Sinister) side of the body was associated with evil; right-hand 'Dexter' = good.*

4. That it alludes to the typical dress of a medieval apprentice – knee length britches and an open 'V' necked shirt.

5. Medieval folk also covered up skin blemishes for fear of being misdiagnosed as Lepers – It is possible that Candidates exhibited their skin as one of the proofs of fitness.

6. Exposure of the leg to show the absence of leg iron markings – further evidence of being free.

Lastly, we come to our neck apparel, the original purpose of which is fully explored in the *Medieval Apprentices and their Masters* section, as is the importance of unblemished skin. One thing to say is that the cable-tow has no connection with a hangman's noose, rather it served very practical purposes on medieval building sites and quarries. In English Freemasonry the cable-tow is not generally accorded any symbolic value, but some Brethren take it to imply 'ignorance arising from bondage'. For example, in medieval times the majority of Serfs were bound to the land controlled by a Feudal Lord and were not really free to think or act for themselves. They were effectively enslaved.

The practical ceremonial application of the cable-tow was simply that of controlling Candidates. In other Masonic jurisdictions there are several differing symbolic interpretations including umbilical cord (rebirth); connection to God; submission to judgement; pledging one's life; bond of love etc. These are listed to simply illustrate the diversity of symbolic interpretations in the global fraternity that is Freemasonry.

**Overview:** We are prepared for Masonic rebirth in both mind and body; our senses are being tested to prove fitness: our sensory perception is limited sharpening our concentration; we have nothing of value – we are transiting from a materialistic world to embrace a more spiritually founded, gentle Masonic philosophy; we are not in control of events and are dependent on the services of our conductor – a truly humbling, character testing experience.

## 2]    Admission - into the Lodge

At the Lodge door we heard how the Tyler summoned the attention of those in the Lodge room (3) which shortly received a response. The Tyler having stated our credentials for admission '...free and of good report', effectively the Degree's password, the door closes shortly to reopen again. We are welcomed into the Lodge by the Inner Guard who pointedly reminded us of the seriousness of what was to ensue (testing our senses of hearing and touch)

Our conductor, the Junior Deacon, instructs us to lead off with our left (Latin: sinister) foot which can be interpreted as trampling evil underfoot, guiding us a short distance and then halts. The next voice we heard was that of the Worshipful Master who put two confirmatory questions to us regarding the status of our liberty and age.

The historical context of being 'free' is explored in the *Medieval Apprentices and their Masters* section, but there is another application that needs to be considered. Those first free thinkers who established Speculative Freemasonry recognised the philosophical principle that physical freedom and the freedom to think for oneself were inextricably linked. Anyone, for whatever reason, who had their liberty constrained was consequently not in a position to embrace, practise and benefit from Masonic principles. (In a similar vein, the Worshipful Master later enquires if we have been pressurised into joining Freemasonry).

Questions answered, a Prayer ensues – all medieval ceremonies had a prayer – a point also echoed by the Lodge Openings and Closings. Our belief in a Supreme Being is then questioned, confirmed and rewarded by the reassurance that we will be safely conducted around the Lodge.

## 3]    Pass before the Brethren

Sometimes referred to as 'Circumambulation' – contextual meaning 'to ceremoniously walk around the Lodge'. This should not be confused with the term 'Perambulate' which simply means 'to walk around'.

As we begin moving around the Lodge room, we increasingly came to appreciate the guidance and support provided by our Conductor, the Junior Deacon [JD] . We pass before the Brethren so they can see that we are 'fit and properly prepared'. However, our medieval forebears would have had a very keen interest in the skin condition of every Candidate – as will be later discovered in the *Medieval Apprentices and their Masters* section. Having a skin scarring condition such as acne 600 years ago could have been highly problematical for any aspiring Candidate!

One way of making sense of what happens next is to think of the three Principal Officers (3) – the Worshipful Master (WM) the Senior & Junior Wardens (SW & JW respectively) – each holding a symbolic spiritual representation. The JW representing the physical 'Body'; the SW the 'Soul' and the WM the 'Spirit'. (3) The JW (Body) enquires about our qualifications with the JD answering on our behalf; satisfied we are permitted to enter (pass). This instantly proposes a question – if we are already in the Lodge room what have we actually been permitted to enter? The answer is we are symbolically about to enter King Solomon's Temple. In some European jurisdictions, the two Wardens sit together in the West (e.g. Austria) based on a belief that during the heat of the day the two original Wardens sat side-by-side, each in the shadow of one of the two pillars at the entrance of KST.

**Note:** *A ritual custodian of a 18th century Masonic Ceremony demonstration team advises that, for this reason, 18th century Deacons would have approached the Wardens from behind their chairs to shoulder alert them.*

We then progressed to the SW (Soul) who similarly qualified us before likewise permitting us to enter. (At this point we had symbolically moved between the two Pillars at the entrance of KST which are represented on or close to the Warden's pedestals. We had not yet entered the Temple). The SW (Soul) then informed the WM (Spirit) who was situated within the Porchway that we are in a state of readiness to be reborn into Masonic life, that is to say, 'properly prepared' in mind and body. As a precautionary check, the WM asked a series of questions directed at ensuring that we are truly entering Freemasonry of our own free will and accord. Duly satisfied, the WM commanded that we be instructed to advance to the pedestal; in doing so we symbolically entered the Porchway of KST.

## 4]    Advancing to the Pedestal

The JD gave us explicit three-stage instructions (3) as to how to complete this journey noting the varying 'irregular' lengths of movement, leading off with our left foot to symbolically trample upon evil. The movements allude to the unregulated nature of our non-Masonic lives, before taking our 'First Regular Step' into our new life as a Freemason. A deeper, spiritual interpretation is that of our body, soul and spirit, separately stepping out of the irregular world, ready to commit to a higher level of moral consciousness, symbolised by the formation of a Square. Yet, there is even more symbolism being expressed.

These three movements take us to the East where our Masonic life journey is about to begin. They represented the three sides of a triangle (3) with one angle being a perfect right-angle of 90 degrees. The sides of such a right-angled triangle are always in proportion to the ratio of 3-4-5 originally symbolising 'perfection' and 'Deity'; more recently in Freemasonry 'Universal Nature', with 'Deity' symbolised by an equilateral triangle.

Ritual practised by the Antients Lodges was generally longer and more detailed than present day Emulation Ritual. For example, when advancing to the pedestal the JD specified the distances in inches to be taken for each movement – the sequential distances of 9, 12 and 15 inches are fully compliant with the Pythagorean 3-4-5 ratio.

At school we most likely encountered this ratio as Pythagoras' Theorem, but it is also known as the 47th Problem of Euclid, or Euclid's 47th Proposition. Its import to both Operative and Speculative Freemasons is that it is the founding calculation of geometrical architectural design dating back to ancient Egypt. In ancient times it was also been taken to represent 'Deity'. From this single element of mathematical knowledge, perfectly formed right-angled triangles, squares and circles can be drawn or set out on the ground. The Master Mason Architects who

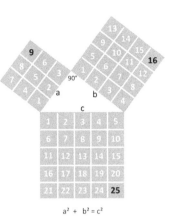

$$a^2 + b^2 = c^2$$

designed our stunning medieval cathedrals did so using nothing more than these simple shapes. Every single building starts with the formation of a perfect right-angle to site the foundation stone. The ability to form a perfect right-angle means we also have the capacity to form a perfect Square. As a whole, the advancement communicated to the WM that with the help of God we were ready to build a new, Masonic life. We will return to the 3-4-5 ratio later in the Ceremony when in the North East part of the Lodge.

## 5]    Obligation

Then standing in the East, the WM explained the principles of Freemasonry confirming their compatibility with our religious beliefs and the conduct of everyday life. We were then directly asked if we were willing to take a Solemn Obligation and promise to maintain secrecy. Strictly speaking, we should have answered this question without any prompting – it ought to come from our heart, ideally without any third party influence or direction. Accordingly, Emulation Ritual directs that the JD should wait to see if the Candidate answers spontaneously before prompting.

On receiving our consent, the WM gave instructions concerning the position to be adopted for taking the Obligation. Our flesh was exposed to the kneeling stool and VSL, and our heart (naked left breast) is pointedly reminded again of the seriousness of the occasion.

The Obligation is effectively a lifelong pledge of concealment, specifically not to disclose the secrets and mysteries of Ancient Freemasonry, which we will not write or record in any way. Bearing in mind that since 1969 Emulation Ritual has been recorded in writing – what do we actually need to keep secret and not recorded in any way? Fortunately, this has been clarified by Grand

Lodge as being the Sign, Token and Word entrusted to us after we have been Obligated. However, this proposes another question, as it takes just a minute of Internet searching to find a written record of our secrets. So, if everything is out in the public domain, why bother honouring our Obligation? The answer is that each of us honours it as a collective demonstration of mutual trust – it holds great significance and importance to us as Freemasons, and to us as Freemasons alone.

If we think about our medieval Apprenticed forebears, were they given instruction in the secrets of the Masonry trade? Were there any such secrets

to impart? We do not know, but if there were, and say a non-Mason discovered a trade secret through devious means what were the real world consequences? The recipient of that information had neither the tools, nor the training to exploit that knowledge, assuming they understood it in the first place. The same principle applies to our Masonic secrets – the maintenance of secrecy only means something to us – the wider world does not have the Masonic teachings and tools to make any sense of our secrets. As previously mentioned, the real Masonic secrets are those discoveries we make about ourselves in our ongoing Masonic quest for self-improvement.

It is clear from medieval records that Apprentices of all trades memorised their Obligations; there are also some 15th century records (not Masonry) of some Apprentices being able to write their Obligations – due to a progressive improvement in literacy during the preceding two centuries. Under the English Constitution, some Lodges still invite their Entered Apprentices to recite their Obligation from memory before being Passed as a Fellow Craft.

Before moving on from the Obligation, we need to acknowledge that its language is archaic, also employing some words and phrases that are peculiar to Freemasonry. In the interest of dispelling the mists of confusion an extensive First Degree glossary forms Part 5 of this book.

## 6] The moment Masonic life begins – Greater & Lesser Lights

The instant we sealed our Obligation on the VSL was the exact moment of our rebirth as an Entered Apprentice Freemason [EAFM] and we were shortly restored to the blessing of Light. The WM wasted no time in starting our Masonic education by both showing and explaining to us the three Great Emblematical Lights (guides) of Freemasonry (3), being the Volume of the Sacred Law (VSL), the Square and Compasses. The VSL governs our faith; the Square symbolically reminds us to check and regulate our behaviour and the Compasses govern our relationship with all humankind. In Freemasonry, the term 'light' can also be taken to mean 'knowledge'.

We were then moved to a position where we could observe (for the first time) the full length of the Lodge Room enabling the WM to point out the Lesser Lights. In English Freemasonry the three Lesser Lights (3) are usually placed on, or are close to, the pedestals of the three Principal Officers, taking the form of real or faux candles. In many other constitutions the three lights (candles) are displayed on an altar, arranged in triangular form.

Collectively, the three lights represent 'The Great Architect of the Universe'.

The present day explanation is that 'the Sun is to rule the day, the Moon to govern the night and the Master to rule and direct his Lodge'. The Master is in the East, the Sun in the West (Senior Warden) and the Moon in the South (Junior Warden) However, it appears the reference to the Worshipful Master is a later replacement for Mercury – the closest planet to the Sun. The reason for this substitution is unknown, but may be connected to the right-angled triangle:

The two sides forming the right-angle represented the Sun (male) and the Moon (female) with Mercury (prodigy) represented by the hypotenuse. This mirrors the values attributed by the Ancient Egyptians to the right-angled triangle – the shortest (female) side represented one of the greatest Egyptian goddesses Isis, goddess of life and magic. Isis married her brother Osiris, represented by the next longest side (male) and their union produced a son Horus, represented by the longest, hypotenuse side (prodigy).

Ancient civilisations worshipped both the Sun and the Moon which symbolised the struggles between day and night, good and evil, etc. This enduring theme has been reinterpreted throughout the ages – including Freemasonry's Lesser Lights which allude to God. They do so because a triangle, composed of three straight lines, has no discernible beginning or end. There is no connection with the Holy Trinity.

## 7]    Physical Penalties & Entrustment

Having taken the first regular step and properly advanced to the WM, the cable-tow was removed and passed to the WM. In some overseas Masonic jurisdictions this is the moment when the umbilical cord is symbolically cut. Having been informed of the physical penalties, it came as some relief that these are symbolic and deemed unnecessary and are consequently no longer included in the Obligation. The Ritual workings practised by some Masonic jurisdictions have never included any physical penalties whilst others have subsequently removed them. These penalties seem to be later additions to the Ceremony given that the Old Charges, such as those described in the Regius Poem, make no mention of such punitive measures. It appears that medieval Masters were more concerned about their Apprentices damaging their reputations by gossiping about them in public. More about that later.

The WM then instructed us how to identify ourselves to one another as Masons by entrusting us with the Sign, Token and Word of the Degree. These are the secrets we obligate ourselves to keep as a collective responsibility and mutual bond of trust – we never use or disclose these secrets unless we are in attendance of an official Lodge Meeting (practising the Sign unobserved at home is OK). If visiting a Lodge where we are unknown, we should expect the Junior Warden to 'Prove' us by testing our Masonic knowledge including the secrets of those Degrees we are qualified for.

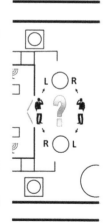

Regarding King's Solomon's Temple, it is important to know where we were standing to determine where Left and Right are. We were symbolically within the entrance of KST (not outside looking in) when the WM, having entrusted us with the secrets of an EAFM, explained the significance of the left -hand pillar which is represented by that column on or close to the JW's pedestal – this is to the left of the representation of the second, partner pillar located on the SW's pedestal.

## 8]    Testing by Junior & Senior Wardens

Prompted by the JD, we demonstrated and repeated our newly acquired secret knowledge to the WM. We were then conducted to the JW who tests our recall of the newly entrusted secrets – we are prompted throughout by the JD. Having passed the test, we were conducted to the SW for a more extensive test, being prompted for a third time [3]. The repetition is clearly intended to deepen our memory and recall of the secrets and their symbolic meanings. There is a considerable responsibility placed upon the Wardens and JD to identify and correct any defects exhibited by Candidates.

## 9]    Apron Investiture

Having passed these tests, the SW presented us to the WM who then commanded that we be invested with the distinguishing badge of an EAFM, a white apron traditionally made from lambskin. White denotes 'purity' and a lamb 'innocence'. The apron is referred to as a 'badge' because it visibly identifies us as an EAFM.

The 1898 publication of *The Man of Mt. Moriah* by Clarence Miles Boutelle recounts a legendary story of the building of King Solomon's Temple, as told by its architect. The legend states that the Masons appointed to build the Temple each sacrificed a lamb, as a symbol of innocence. The carcasses were consumed except for the lambskins which were retained and made into aprons for the Masons to wear. We should not lose sight of the point that this is but a legend.

We were informed that the badge is older and more honourable than the Golden Fleece, the Roman Eagle and Order of the Garter. We need to remember that our Ceremony is being symbolically conducted within the entrance of King Solomon's Temple which was completed around 960 BCE or possibly a little later. Rome was not founded until more than 200 years later in 753 BCE; the quest undertaken  by Jason and the Argonauts for the Golden Fleece is similarly placed in the 8th century BCE; the Order of the Garter was established by Edward III, King of England in 1348 CE and still exists today.

In ancient times people dressed in white robes to signify innocence and purity; indeed, the word 'Candidate' stems from the Latin root of **'candidatus'** which originally meant, 'one clothed in white robes.'

In English Freemasonry, the EA Apron is rectangular in shape being between 14-16 inches wide and 12-14 inches deep, fitted with white strings and a triangular flap. In some Jurisdictions the apron is perfectly square. Many symbolic values have been attributed to the EAFM's apron – here follows some drawn from several Masonic Jurisdictions:

- The four corners denoting Purity, Truth, Sincerity and Honesty.

- The four sides denoting Prudence, Temperance, Fortitude and Justice.

- The three sides of the triangular flap (3) remind us to provide relief to those in distress; treat all those we meet with kindness and friendliness. Similarly, denotes the eternal nature of the Great Architect of the Universe with the three sides representing *Past, Present* and *Future* (3).

- The triangular flap, if worn pointing upwards (some Lodges leave the flap pointing down) denotes that we have yet to be fully invested with Divine wisdom. Alternatively, the elevated triangular flap representing the element Fire, indicating that the blessing of material light has been restored to the wearer, thereby enabling their eyes to perceive Freemasonry's symbolism .

- The circle formed by tying the apron's strings denotes the Spirit.

Whilst our ancient Operative forebears wore aprons to protect their clothing, as Speculative Masons we don aprons to protect our character.

While on the subject of white coloured Masonic attire, medieval masons wore leather gloves (and gauntlets) primarily to protect their hands and lower arms from the corrosive nature of the lime based mortar which bleached the leather white. In order for lime to acquire the adhesive qualities of cement it has to be fired in a kiln to render it into quicklime. Masters were responsible for providing their Apprentices such gloves who were instructed not to lay stones with unfired lime. In some Masonic Jurisdictions, the potential for this oversight forms a symbolic teaching theme.

As we can see, there is an abundance of Masonic symbolism for us to contemplate. On occasions we might find that there is simply too much. Just a reminder that Freemasonry is a personal journey – we should work with those symbols and explanations that we most readily identify with. Masonic symbolism has kaleidoscopic qualities – we have the same instrument holding the same crystals yet the images we each perceive is subject to some variation. Our personal interpretations of Masonry's symbolism will inevitably be subject to some of these variations, making our experience of them unique. However, those three great founding principles of Brotherly Love, Relief and Truth (3) always hold true and are never compromised.

After we had been invested with our white apron, the WM informed us how we are to manage any interpersonal conflicts, so as not to disturb the peace and harmony of the Lodge. Given the quiet, spiritual nature of Freemasonry, preserving the peace and harmony of the Lodge is forever paramount. We should not lose sight of the point that one of Freemasonry's original aims was to heal the divisions of a troubled world enabling members to meet as equals.

## 10] Charge in the North East Corner

The WM commanded the JD to conduct us to the NE part of the Lodge where we placed our feet in the form of a square, half framing the Rough Ashlar. As already mentioned, the Rough Ashlar represents us as an unskilled Entered Apprentice, at the very beginning of our Masonic journey, now opening our minds to the refinements of a Masonic education. The Square we formed symbolised the sound regulation of our conduct, character and actions.

In Speculative Freemasonry, the specific siting of a foundation stone in the NE Corner is symbolic. Standing in the NE provides the best vantage point for observing the arc of the sun. The sun rises in the east, arcing through its meridian, to the west where it sets. Similarly, it was widely accepted that knowledge first developed in the east and later spread to the west. The ancient world considered the east to be strongly associated with both material light and the enlightenment of knowledge. Conversely, northern Europe was thought of as a place of darkness – shorter solar days and populated by uncivilised, warring tribes. Starting to build from the NE corner also provided Operative Masons with the optimum amount of daylight to work in.

Standing in the NE symbolises leaving the darkness of the non-Masonic world to enter the light of Freemasonry, there to begin an enlightening journey of self-discovery – metaphorically, for the new Mason to build a life founded on Masonic principles (for which guidance is initially provided) created through their own desire and industry.

Our charitable capacity was then tested to remind us that we left the material world outside the Lodge door to be received into Freemasonry without means. In some ways the whole Ceremony might be considered to be an expression of charity; a new Brother has been brought into the light of Freemasonry by the industry of those Brethren who have memorised and rehearsed the Ceremony's Ritual. That investment of time was not made for their own advantage, but solely for the benefit of Candidates for Freemasonry. Charity comes in many forms – a few words of encouragement and support can give a powerful psychological boost to the recipient of such a kindness.

In laying a foundation or corner stone, our ancient forebears took great trouble in accurately siting the stone. Firstly, they would need to pinpoint with precision where East was; secondly, form a perfectly right-angled corner in the NE and thirdly, mark out the ground. They achieved the first two elements by using four sticks, a length of rope with 12 equal length sections marked on it and the application of the Pythagorean 3-4-5 ratio.

Laying a single stick on the ground they would orientate it to point North/ South by reference to the position of the sun and stars such as Polaris – the North Star.

Placing a second stick upright in the ground near the end of the first stick (does not matter which end) one end of the rope is placed by the erect stick and a line of three units of measurement extended in any direction where the third stick is placed erect in the ground with the rope turned around it; similarly a further line of four units of measurement extended and the fourth stick placed upright in the earth with the remaining string of five units returned to the second stick.

The position of the vertical sticks is adjusted until the full length of the string is deployed in an exact 3-4-5 ratio.

Thus, a right-angled triangle has been perfectly formed that also defines both east and west.

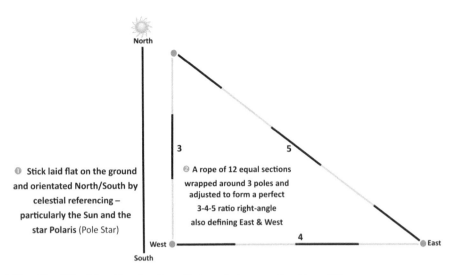

North

South

West

East

3

5

4

① Stick laid flat on the ground and orientated North/South by celestial referencing – particularly the Sun and the star Polaris (Pole Star)

② A rope of 12 equal sections wrapped around 3 poles and adjusted to form a perfect 3-4-5 ratio right-angle also defining East & West

## 11]    The Working Tools of an Entered Apprentice Free Mason

Medieval Apprentices would have worked with tools such as squares, rulers, gauges, gavels and chisels for up to six days of the week, the Sabbath and holidays excepted. They probably only thought about them as work tools and the need to keep them safe and in good repair. Most likely, it was Speculative Freemasons who attached symbolic values to these tools, so once the associated Ritual was competently memorised the intrinsic moral teachings enjoyed an enduring top of mind status. This created a deeper understanding and an 'always on call' memory of the words for future contemplation. As EAFM's we are taught how to employ our time for prayer, work and helping others in need; to manage our thought processes by listening to our conscience, thinking purely and positively. Finally, to expand our knowledge and skills to the best of our ability for the benefit of ourselves and the greater social good.

## 12]    Explanation of the First Degree Tracing Board

In English Freemasonry, this working is generally not included in the Ceremony of Initiation but is sometimes presented during a Regular Meeting. The Ritual is included towards the back of the Emulation Ritual book – a colour image of a First Degree Tracing Board is featured. In other Masonic Jurisdictions such as the USA, such explanations are referred to as 'Lectures'; the corresponding First Degree Tracing Board lecture certainly forms an important part of their Ceremony of Initiation.

In medieval Operative masonry the Tracing Board was used by Masters to draw architectural designs which were then traced onto cloth fabric. The cloth tracings were cut out and trimmed – rather like a tailor cutting cloth for a suit – to create a template for the masons to follow. Complex shapes had multiple templates which were assembled to render a 3D model. Please refer to the *Medieval Apprentices and their Masters* section to discover which two English cathedrals still have their original Tracing Board medium.

In Speculative Craft Masonry there are three Tracing Boards (3) one for each Degree which are usually housed in a plan chest and/or secreted behind shutters on the WM's and Warden's pedestals. Each board serves rather like an allegorical story board, rich in symbolism, used by the WM and other experienced Brethren to give instruction to junior Brethren.

## 13]    The Lodge Warrant

Following an explanation of the Working Tools, the WM called our attention to the Lodge Warrant issued by Grand Lodge. The Warrant is openly displayed during Lodge meetings, so any Brother present can examine it. During the course of our Ceremony of Initiation we would have heard and repeated the phrase 'Just, Perfect and Regular'. The open Volume of the Sacred Law makes the Lodge 'just' (correct); no Candidate can be Initiated unless there are a minimum of seven regularly made Masons in attendance, such minimum attendance makes the Lodge 'perfect' and the display of the Lodge's Warrant (issued by Grand Lodge) makes it 'regular'. We should all make a point of examining our Lodge's Warrant.

We probably received from the WM a copy of the *Book of Constitutions*, which is the successor to the Old Charges previously referred to, and a copy of the Lodge byelaws. At this juncture, the WM invited us to retire from the Lodge to restore our personal comforts, advising us that on our return our attention would be called to an ancient Charge.

## 14]    Charge after Initiation

According to Emulation Ritual, this working should be presented by the WM but in practise is often delegated to a Past Master of the Lodge or a Bro Warden  and more recently, as a Ritual team based presentation. The Charge maps out how we should live our lives as Freemasons. It is quite a lot to take in and it provides an ideal discussion document for mentoring purposes.

Opposite is a key point summary of the Charge in everyday language:

- We were reminded to be guided by the teachings of the VSL – discharging our duties to the Great Architect of the Universe, our fellow humans and ourselves. By honouring the Great Architect in everything we do; by treating our fellow humans respectfully as equals; helping those in need to secure a better future and to maximise our potential to serve the greater good.

- To honour and obey the law of the land, wherever we are in the world, and in all circumstances, remain loyal to the Sovereign of our native country.

- To exercise Wisdom, Moderation, Courage and Fairness in all our undertakings.

- To help those less fortunate than ourselves through acts of charity, kindness, support and assistance.

- As Freemasons, resolutely to keep those Secrets entrusted to us; to demonstrate our Fidelity (loyalty) by never seeking out (e.g. Internet searches) the secrets of superior Degrees and not to recommend anyone as a Candidate for Freemasonry who is unlikely to appreciate and follow Masonic ideology; faithfully to observe all the rules and regulations of Craft Freemasonry including attending Lodge when summoned; behaving modestly; never discussing either politics or religion during meetings; accepting all resolutions formally approved by a majority of Brethren and obey the commands of the WM and Brother Wardens when acting within the remit of their authority. To undertake positive, socially beneficial actions to gain the respect of others and enhance the standing of Freemasonry.

- To continue our quest for Masonic knowledge on a daily basis. (Without compromising our work or family life)

The WM informed us that our Ceremony of Initiation was complete and commanded the JD to conduct us to our seat in the Lodge.


The following *Medieval Apprentices and their Masters* section is intended to provide colour and context of Freemasonry's historical roots – trusting it further invokes a profound sense of belonging to something very special.

# Medieval Apprentices and their Masters

**Introduction:** Whilst we know very little about medieval Ceremonies of Initiation for 13th-15th century Masons, the following general interest notes are solely intended to provoke reflection and discussion.

**Feudal System:** Following the Norman Conquest, William the Conqueror granted usage and management of the land to his 'tenants-in-chief'; specifically, Dukes, Earls and Barons who swore allegiance to him, promising to raise men at arms during times of war. Knights similarly pledged themselves as defenders of the realm, often holding land as a Vassal (land manager) from a tenant-in-chief. On a similar basis, Squires and Gentlemen also held smaller, manorial parcels of land. Collectively, this was a very small 'power holding' group accounting for less than 1% of England's population.

There was a multitude of ecclesiastical office holders including Archbishops, Bishops, Abbots, Canons, Archdeacons, Priors, Rectors, Vicars, Friars and other lesser posts. If you did not have a sword by your side or spend much of your day on your knees in prayer, you would most likely have been a Peasant, either working the land as a Serf or self-employed as a Freeman.

**Serfs:** Were effectively enslaved being granted land for subsistence farming and a hovel to live in. In exchange, a typical Serf worked (unpaid) 3-4 days on his feudal lord's land leaving 2-3 days for working his own plot and a day for the Sabbath. Serfs were not permitted to sell their land; their feudal Lords or Vassals could not sell them without also selling the land to which they were attached. The children of Serfs automatically entered Serfdom under the same terms as their parents. Serfs were further subdivided into *Villeins*, *Half-Villeins* and *Cottagers* each with differing land rights and constraints on their liberty. They usually only married someone within their manorial domain to avoid inter-manorial disputes as to who feudally held sway over any children.

Serfs were generally highly religious, forming small communities and were keen supporters of their local church. Young Serfs sometimes ran away to a city or market town to try and establish themselves as Freemen by seeking out a trade apprenticeship or paid employment. Those who were caught were severely punished, returned to Serfdom, often losing their livelihoods.

**Freemen:** Generally leased small parcels of land and property which they farmed or worked a trade from for profit. Strictly speaking, only the children of Freemen could take on an apprenticeship although the vocational opportunities for girls were fairly limited. Freemen aspired to help healthy sons to become successful businessmen by securing merchant or trade apprenticeships through social and familial networking. As family lines often petered out, much parental thought was applied to helping healthy children to make something of themselves. Unlike Serfs, Freemen and their families were 'free' to travel.

**Towns & Cities:** By the 14th century between 10% and 15% of the population lived in a large town or city – everyone else lived in a rural setting. However, we should not lose sight of the considerable numbers of visitors drawn into the bustling urban environments, predominantly to trade, or break a journey. Towns and cities had quickly evolved as vibrant administrative and economic centres for a wide range of merchant and craft trades including masonry. Many Master Mason businessmen were already appreciating the virtues of coming together under the geographical umbrella of a urban Guild, drawing sons of rural Freemen to be apprenticed. Most Master Masons would have probably only trained one or two Apprentices during their relatively short working lives of 20 years or so – and even if they had a son of the right age, he may have been in poor health.

**The Medieval Dream:** The broad, medieval dream for the son of a Freeman was to leave the countryside, serve an urban apprenticeship, earn and/or inherit enough money to set up his own business as a Master; enjoy prosperity; return to the countryside as a member of the landed gentry; spend a long retirement waited on by servants; die a painless death and, as a devoted, alms giving, servant of God, pass very quickly through purgatory to take up permanent residence in heaven!

Today, we are familiar with a similar cycle of young people being drawn to the cities and larger towns to work, prosper and eventually retire to a more tranquil, pastoral setting. The main difference nowadays is that those so blessed have virtually a whole world to choose from.

**Candidates for Apprenticeship:** For a Master seeking the ideal Apprentice, the first requirement was to ensure that the candidate was the son of a Freeman. Inadvertently taking on any other class of Serf was disastrous if discovered – the Serf's Feudal Lord simply claimed his man back, no matter if the

the young man was in his final year of apprenticeship, the Law was on the Feudal Lord's side. Thinking back to the Ceremony of Initiation, we were all asked by the WM if we are a free man.

**Interviews:** A worldly wise Master interviewed not just the Candidate and his parents, but also the family's friends, one of whom may have initially proposed or sponsored the Candidate to the Master. A diligent Master would have been keenly interested in how the prospective candidate had been brought up; how any older siblings had turned out in terms of character, physique and temperament whilst assessing if the parenting of the son ideologically coincided with his own views. The candidate's parents would have initially put out feelers via their social and familial networks to try and identify a Master looking for a new Apprentice. They did not generally specify a particular trade or vocation, as long as it was judged desirable and honourable. An apprenticed Mason recruited in this way usually entered the Craft opportunistically and not by exercising vocational choice. The Guild's Wardens would also have been involved in the interview process which almost certainly included a physical examination of the Candidate.

**Matrimony:** Nearly everyone would expect to be married – the long-lived (particularly women) could reasonably expect to be married at least twice. It was possible to marry as soon as puberty was reached – girls from the age of 12 years and boys from about the age of 15 years. However, in practice the first marriage was arranged, typically between a well off older man and a much younger girl. This was very much the accepted practice as it yielded practical advantages. The older man knew that his young wife would outlive him; he would bequeath or gift to her and any surviving children a substantial part of the wealth he had accumulated over his lifetime; he fully expected her to remarry after his death. Serfs could usually only marry someone within their manorial domain to avoid inter-manorial disputes as to who held sway over any children, but for the sons and daughters of Freemen, things could be markedly different. However, apprenticed young men could not marry.

**Moral Integrity:** Like father, like son? Honesty, personal integrity, trustworthiness, politeness and good manners were all positive traits looked for in the ideal Apprentice. For the Master and his Guild these qualities would have ranked very highly for slightly differing reasons. The Master was going to bring a new member into his household for a minimum of seven years, so it was crucial that the young man jogged along amicably with everyone else. If an older Master had taken a much younger wife (as young as 12 years old, but more likely a little older) bringing a boy of similar age into the household, on the cusp of adolescence, does not seem to be particularly wise. However, the Master might have looked upon his Apprentice as his potential successor in both business and matrimony. In this way he might exercise some control over his legacy, trusting the Apprentice, once married to his widow, would instruct any surviving sons in the Craft. A younger Master with daughters might take a similar view, this time evaluating a Candidate as a prospective son-in-law.

Guilds were also highly supportive of a deceased member's widow remarrying another Guild member. If the deceased Master had an Apprentice, his widow inherited the contract to train him. Who was going to continue to run the business of the deceased Master and train his Apprentice? Perhaps there was a qualified mason ripe for marriage and/or advancement to Master Mason status either within the existing business or within the Guild's wider membership. Again, when it came to medieval marriage, the harsh practicalities of life tended to overrule the directives of the heart.

From the Guild's perspective, the largest masonry customer groups of the period, by a very long way, were the Church and the Crown, both demanding the highest standards of workforce integrity. Indeed, on major ecclesiastical building projects the Church sometimes required the Master Mason architect to take an Obligation that he would oversee the moral conduct and welfare of the workforce, punishing any transgressor who stepped out of line. In some instances, the Church appointed a cleric to oversee the moral behaviour and welfare of the workforce, effectively working alongside the Master Mason architect. The bottom line is that neither the Master, nor the Guild wished to take on the hot headed as Apprentices – unfortunately the unpredictable nature of adolescence often frustrated their best intentions. This probably helped the early Guilds come to recognise the potential of education as a desirable, calming influence.

**Candidates skin condition:** Life in 14th century England could be very short – infant mortality was incredibly high as immature immune systems contended with many life threatening infections such as Cholera, Typhoid, Typhus, Leprosy, Chicken Pox, Smallpox, Diphtheria, Measles etc. Even in normal circumstances, half of the infants born would not survive into adolescence. If a young man got to the age of 20 years, the prospect of his surviving to celebrate his 40th birthday was good but was by no means guaranteed. The stark medieval reality was that death was omnipresent, so life was for living and each day well lived was a celebration of an answered prayer.

Prior to 1346, when the Plague first arrived in England, the most feared medieval disease was Leprosy. The progress of this disease is very slow – an initial, gradual loss of sensation in the extremities ultimately leading to their paralysis and ulceration. After a couple of years, fingers and toes drop off, body hair is lost, facial features – particularly the nose – begin to lose definition, seemingly melting away. Progressive ulceration, with all the attendant unpleasant odours, also caused blindness. The afflicted simply rotted away over a lengthy period of time – it was literally thought of as a living death inflicted by God as a severe punishment for a serious wrongdoing.

Such was the level of fear that any skin conditions causing long-term scarring, such as acne, dermatitis, eczema, psoriasis etc were readily deemed to be symptomatic of the onset of Leprosy and often misdiagnosed as such. Consequently, those afflicted with such conditions kept their blemishes covered up and/or disguised the affected skin in some way. Once correctly or wrongly diagnosed, the Church ordered that each Leper be shunned, cloaked and provided with a bell to be sounded to warn the 'healthy' of their approach. Leprosy was seen as God's punishment of a serious sinner, hence the involvement of the Church in the management of the afflicted.

**Candidate's Physique:** The adjective 'lithe' regularly occurs in medieval records as the ideal physique for 13-15 year old male trade apprentices. Again, some judgement had to be made about a boy's potential physical strength in manhood. People of the time well understood the concept of 'the runt of the litter' and happily applied it in a human context. So, how on earth did a Master make a judgement over such matters? It seems reasonable to infer that there must have been a physical examination of the Candidate, probably by Guild's Wardens, as part of an overall 'fitness' assessment.

Again, the physique of any older brothers would have been considered. Coincidentally, a Knight's physique would have dwarfed that of a medieval worker – due to better health, diet and genetic disposition afforded by the tendency for the 'bigger bodied' elite to intermarry. Size mattered, so a boy of above average size for his age and 'lithe' would have caught any Master's eye.

**The Plague:** The first European plague pandemic arrived in England in 1346, and did not abate until 1350 – It is estimated that 30% to 60% of Europe's population perished during the first pandemic. From around the year 1050, Europe experienced a 250 year long warm epoch fuelling a population explosion. A more populous Europe needed to be fed, triggering large scale land clearances to create the requisite agricultural capacity. A rapidly growing population also demanded more imported goods and merchants consequently commissioned the construction of increasingly larger merchant ships. We now know that the plague bacterium was transmitted by fleas carried by black rats (aka ship rats) but this was unknown at the time. Worst scenario estimates imply that England's pre-pandemic population of around 6 million souls declined over the ensuing 4-5 years to around 2.5 million. To describe the impact as devastating comes nowhere close to defining what must have been a 'living hell on earth'. Building works came to a standstill.

Given that the Church had positioned such diseases as God's punishment for sinning, people demanded to know why so many innocents had died. Survivors would have experienced around half the people they knew simply being wiped off the face of the earth over a four year period. The Church made no response to this fundamental question of faith – the void of silence was therefore filled by the conspiracy theories of the common folk. In many parts of Europe, the Jews were blamed, accused of poisoning the wells and were consequently murdered in great numbers. In other parts, Lepers were blamed and likewise murdered along with those afflicted with acne, dermatitis, eczema and other scarring skin disorders. Thereafter, the Plague reared its ugly head every 20-30 years in England, particularly in London where 10%-20% of the population routinely perished with each outbreak – it was a morbid fear with a grip that never completely went away.

We all made certain adjustments to our clothing whilst preparing for our Ceremony of Initiation. The founding reason for this requirement is not fully understood – there are various opinions including to show proof of gender; prove the absence of hidden weaponry, whilst others say it is to bring the candidate's exposed skin into contact with the Lodge, or to mimic medieval dress. There has also been academic speculation that, at some time in the past, medieval Candidates were Initiated in a state of complete undress, symbolically representing rebirth. The honest answer is that we do not know why such preparations came about. We certainly know that medieval Ceremonies of Initiation were intended to make a dramatic and lasting impression on the Candidate's mind. We can also have a high degree of confidence that both the Master and his Guild would only wish to take on lithe and healthy Apprentices, so it is feasible that Candidates had to show proof of being free from Leprosy and/or the Plague (and the other misdiagnosed skin conditions) by exhibiting some or all of their skin, prior to, and/or during their Ceremonies of Initiation.

**Rope and the Cable-tow:** There would have been plenty of rope on a medieval building site, predominantly used for lifting and dragging heavy stones and other materials; binding wooden scaffolding etc. From the construction of Egypt's Pyramids to the building of our Medieval cathedrals, large, finished stones would have been transported, from quarry to site, on river borne rafts or boats. Those vessels would have been manoeuvred, guided, towed and held in station for loading and unloading from the riverbank by the attachment of rope cables. No doubt, manoeuvring such a heavily laden raft would have required many hands and cable-tows of varying lengths. According to *Mackey's Encyclopaedia of Freemasonry*, cable-tow is probably derived from the German for cable or rope, *'kabeltauw'*. Other scholars point to alternative roots such as Hebrew *'Khabel'* or Dutch *'cabel'*.

One of the oldest knots is the Bowline, said to have been used by the gangs of Egyptian pyramid builders, it is routinely used for lifting heavy loads; is very easy to tie and untie onehandedly, even after having taken a heavy load. There is a medieval story explaining how to tie a Bowline knot. Take a length of rope, ❶ creating a loop (rabbit hole) towards the top leaving a foot or so of rope above the hole (a tree). The bottom end of the rope is the rabbit; ❷ the rabbit runs up through the rabbit hole; ❸ round the back of the tree and back down the hole. ❹ Tighten and that is it – an ancient Bowline knot. A derivative form of this knot is the Running Bowline which creates a running noose from a double rabbit hole. As Apprentices, every medieval Mason would have been taught to how to tie both these knots.

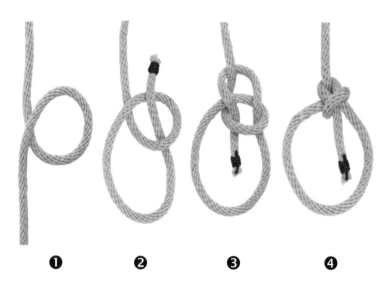

❶          ❷          ❸          ❹

**Contracting in the 15th century:** There are several biblical references to the symbolic removal of a sandal to publicly signify the sealing of a contract. The single sandal or shoe was openly removed by the vendor and temporarily passed to the purchaser; today we would simply shake hands on a deal to symbolise mutual acquiescence. The removal of a sandal or shoe took its rise from ancient land transactions signifying the purchaser of the land is now entitled to step onto the land as its new owner. One biblical reference to the removal of a sandal relates to such a land purchase that led to the marriage of Boaz and Ruth. (Ruth 4 v 1-17)

This practice appears to have followed through into the Middle Ages, for example, the father of a bride might remove one of the bride's shoes and hand it to the groom signifying his consent to the marriage contract.

A 15th century apprenticed Mason would have entered into a contract with his Master quite some time before his Initiation. For the London Masons' Company, the rule was that a Master had a year and a day post contract to formally enter his Apprentice on the Guild's roll. In practice, this seems to have worked as a trial period during which both parties could terminate the contract by mutual consent.

In view of the above, it is feasible that 15th century Initiates removed a shoe to signify either they had already submitted to the terms of an apprenticeship contract, or perhaps more likely, in recognition of the seriousness of the impending Obligation and their submission to it.

**Keeping the peace with swords and daggers:** *The Statute of Winchester* 1285, required every man aged 15 to 60 years to carry weapons in public as a peace keeping initiative. The level of armament varied according to landownership and the income it generated, but even those on modest incomes carried a dagger or sword. Town and city ordinances imposed fines for drawing weapons in a public place without cause, with eye-wateringly high fines for anyone unjustly drawing blood. When attending church meetings or social gatherings all weapons had to be surrendered before entering the principal part of the host building.

Even when Speculative Freemasonry got underway, men were still bearing arms in public; the quality and type of arms carried, and any armour worn disclosed their social standing. As Brothers we are all equal, so disarming for Lodge meetings also maintained the egalitarian status quo.

**Metal & Money:** Before 1694 there were no bank notes, just coins generally made from silver. Paper money was first introduced as promissory notes in 1694, when the Bank of England was established, albeit in very high denominations. As metal came from below ground, some would view metallic items with suspicion as it could be associated with the underworld and the devil. However, such qualms did not prevent the large scale mining of some five metals in medieval England namely, tin, copper, silver, iron and lead.

**Left-Handed:** Left-handed (cack-handed) people were not trusted because the left hand was associated with the devil. The Latin for 'right' is Dexter and for 'left' is Sinister; thus, the human body is equally split between good and evil. Leading off with the left foot can be interpreted as 'trampling evil underfoot'.

## Apprenticeship Contract Elements

**Secrecy:** As a member of the household, the Apprentice inevitably became aware of his Master's personal affairs, habits and idiosyncrasies. A gossiping Apprentice could easily damage his Master's social standing and business prospects. For this reason, Apprenticeship contracts generally had a 'Secrecy Clause' which is often considered (perhaps mistakenly) to have included any trade secrets or specialist knowhow shared with the Apprentice. We do not really know the details of any such trade secrets, or whether any actually existed. Even if trade secrets did exist, their disclosure would have been meaningless to anyone without the tools and training to exploit them. Gossiping was also a minor medieval crime punishable by extra work, a fine or time in the stocks. The ability to keep secrets was therefore an imperative.

**Sobriety, Gambling & Cuckolding:** Apprenticeship contracts usually specified that the Apprentice was not to frequent taverns, theatres etc. or participate in games of chance, such as dice. They also forbade intimate relationships with the opposite sex, both within and outside of the Master's household – such relationships outside marriage would have been unlawful at the time. The Master, in many respects, became the Apprentice's de facto Guardian and as such was entitled to instil compliance with his instructions and contractual rights by the reasonable use of corporal punishment.

**Payments to the Apprentice:** In exchange for his training the Apprentice generally received no monetary payment during the apprenticeship term. Some Masters may have made a small allowance from any wages the Master received for his Apprentice's labours. The Master typically agreed to provide, at his expense, accommodation, clothing (including work gloves and shoes) food and the use of the essential tools. Contracts sometimes specified a small payment to the Apprentice upon the successful completion of his apprenticeship or the gift of tools. The payment may have been intended for the purchase of tools, as Masons seeking employment were expected to provide their own. Sometimes a fixed wage, 1-2 year post apprenticeship term of employment as a bachelor was also included.

Masters often bequeathed tools or small monetary sums to those who worked for them including their Apprentices. This simply may have been to ensure, in the event of their unexpected death, the continuance of any contracted work in progress, so keeping the family business alive.

**Payments to the Master:** Parents usually contracted to pay the Master a specified sum to take their offspring into apprenticeship. Such payments usually obliged the Master to enrol the Apprentice with both the City and Guild institutions for which fees were due and each had a related Ceremony of Initiation. It was not cheap and progressively became dearer over time.

Sometimes a third party stood as Surety for the Apprentice (often his Sponsor) and would be similarly contractually bound to make a compensatory payment to the Master should the Apprentice breach his contract, e.g. if he ran away (a common, homesickness driven occurrence) and failed to return within a reasonable time. It was also possible for the family of a very unhappy Apprentice to buy his contract out from the Master.

**Servitude:** Most contracts specified that the Apprentice was to be instructed in the Mistery (trade) and not to be treated as a general servant, that is to say, running domestic errands, undertaking household chores or working as a Mason's servant (labourer). Notwithstanding, cashflow challenged Masters forced to lay off a valued servant may well have prevailed upon their Apprentice to temporarily fill such voids. The matter really revolved around the quality of their working relationship as to whether compliance resulted. The Apprentice would have been entitled to complain to the Guild which the Wardens would have then investigated, but those in the early years of apprenticeship were often too nervous to act.

**Sickness:** Although not specifically mentioned in contracts, it seems the general practice was that a Master would extend the same level of care to his Apprentice, as he would to any other member of his household. However, an Apprentice would most likely return to his family home to recuperate from any prolonged bout of sickness or incapacitating injury.

**Tracing Board:** The Master Mason architect, charged with building a medieval cathedral, would have based himself in a dedicated building or room forming part of the principal building. This effectively served as his planning office. He drew designs, hosted meetings, commissioned works and ordered supplies from what, in some respects, could be likened to a present day Lodge Room. The room or apartment would have been oblong in shape with much of the centre floor area covered in plaster – there are fine examples of such a room at Wells Cathedral and the Mason's Loft in York Minster.

**Note:** *To book a special guided tour of the latter visit the York Minster website.*

The plastered floor was for drawing designs of most aspects of the building. Once a design had been approved by the building's sponsor, templates for individual stones would have been made by tracing them from the floor designs onto cloth – for an intricate piece of masonry several templates would be required – one for each aspect. These would be scissor cut much in the way a tailor cuts cloth for a suit – the templates could then be folded to make a 3D impression of the work.

*Medieval scissors*

However, the most complex stone carving work could not be designed in this way. To guide the intricate carving of stone animals, human figures, faces etc the 'Imaginers', the most highly skilled Masons, would have been shown an illustration or sketch of the subject matter – a prototype may even have been carved in wood for The Master Mason architect's approval.

Once the floor was full of design workings they were lost as the whole area was simply re-plastered. It was not customary during these times to make a drawn record of the design work. In 'The Master Mason's Loft' at York Minster, a recognisable set of window designs is still visible on the floor based Tracing Board. The margins of the floor also disclose how the plaster surface was smoothed – the patter of children's feet – adults were too heavy and would have left clearly discernible footprints in the wet plaster. Common sense suggests that no one would walk across the Master Mason's floor designs – they would have respectfully walked round the plastered area, similar to 'squaring' the Lodge.

**Medieval Lifting Gear – the Lewis:** Stones were raised to great heights using treadmill powered cranes fashioned from wood, ropes and pulleys. There was also a cramp based lifting system mounted on a tripod called a Lewis – derived from the Latin word 'lueis' which means to levitate. A scaled representation of a Lewis forms part of our Craft Lodge furnishings today, it is usually situated on or in close proximity to the Senior Warden's pedestal. Stones that needed to be raised had a hole bored into the centre of a surface that would not be visible post installation.

A set of Lewis Pins, rather like a pair of inverted callipers, were placed into the aperture and attached to the pulley rope. As the rope tensioned, the jaws of the Lewis Pins opened biting into the sides of the aperture allowing the stone to be slowly and carefully raised. Once the stone was grounded, the pins relaxed and could be readily removed from the stone.

The term 'Lewis' also denotes the son of a present day Freemason who can be Initiated into Freemasonry from the age of 18 years, rather than the customary minimum admission age of 21 years.

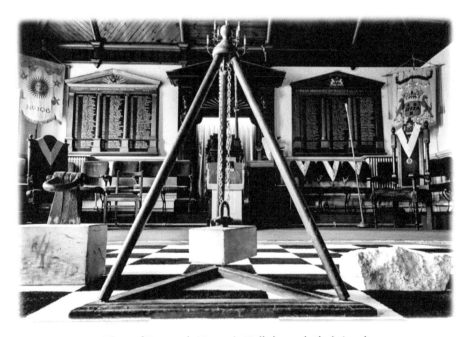

***View of Exmouth Masonic Hall through their Lewis.***
*Image courtesy of Exmouth Masonic Hall, Devon – exmouthfreemasons.org*

**The Square:** Early Medieval Squares would typically be made from wood with the two unequal sides of 3:4 Pythagorean proportion. Routinely employed to 'try' abrasive stone surfaces, Squares would wear down to a point where they could not be relied upon to give a truthful gauge. Consequently, Lodges kept a trusted Perfect Ashlar for the Masons to try (test) their wooden Squares on.

One particularly special Square provides a strong evidential link of Speculative Masonry's historical Operative roots and a profound sense of morality. In the November of 1830 excavations of a venerable bridge spanning the River Shannon in the city of Limerick unearthed an archaeological find known as the 'Baal's Bridge Square'. Made from brass, the artefact was discovered beneath the bridge's foundation stone, implying that its interment must have been deliberate. What makes Baal's Bridge Square so special it that it is dated as 1507 and inscribed, one line per side as per the sketch below.

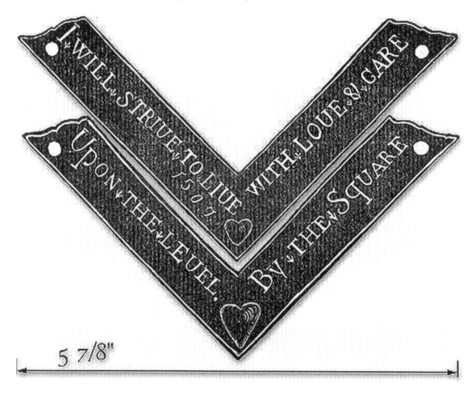

5 7/8"

Above the 'V' of the Square on both sides, a heart shape has been naively engraved. The Square is presently in the safe custody of Antient Union Lodge No 13 in Limerick.

# Part 5

# The First Degree Glossary
*cutting through all the archaic language*

# Glossary *of* Archaic Words & Phrases – *The First Degree*

**Acquiescence:** Consent or agree to.

**Actuated:** In context, 'motivated'.

**Ancient usages and established customs of the Order:** See below.

**Ancient landmarks of the Order:** In ancient times stone pillars (landmarks) denoted territorial boundaries. In Freemasonry, 'ancient landmarks' are its longstanding universal principles, also referred to as *customs and usages* that essentially define Freemasonry, e.g. a belief in a Supreme Being.

**Approbation:** Contextually, this means 'approval'.

**Brotherly love, relief and truth:** In the modern idiom, 'true friendship, supporting those in need and personal integrity'.

**Cable-tow:** Peculiar to Freemasonry, a rope in the form of a running noose placed round a Candidate's neck. Used by medieval masons to control boats or rafts used to transport stones typically from quarry to construction site.

**Cable's length:** Historical definitions range from 3 to 50 miles, the 3 miles thought to be a reasonable walking distance. Also historically used by the British Navy being a length of rope a little over 200 yards. Symbolically, the cable's length represents the extent of our perceived personal responsibility – in the context of our ability to attend Lodge. The length is therefore a variable and a matter of conscience influenced by work, health, family demands etc.

**Common Gavel and Chisel:** A wooden mallet type tool used with a chisel – gently tapping the handle end of the chisel to refine stone surfaces.

**Compasses:** A hinged drawing/measuring instrument comprising a handle and two legs, each terminating in a fine point. They remind us to ferment good relationships with all humankind, particularly our fellow Freemasons.

**Connections:** Immediate family members – spouse, partner, children etc.

**Conduce:** To help bring about an outcome or result.

**Constitution of the Fraternity:** Governing rules — the *Book of Constitutions*

**Corporeal**: Being of the 'body' rather than of the 'spirit' – physical capacity.

**Cowans to Freemasonry:** Historically, a Cowan was a maker of drystone walls who was, in an operative sense, more lowly skilled than a Stone Mason and consequently not qualified to enter a Mason's Lodge. Considered a Scottish term; the *Schaw Statutes of 1598* forbade working with or the hiring of 'cowanis' on a huge penalty of £20. In 1707, Mother Kilwinning Lodge defined a Cowan as a 'Mason without the word'. In a broader, modern Speculative sense, it means anyone who is not a Freemason.

**Daily Advancement: Make a daily advancement in Masonic knowledge:** Spending 5-20 minutes a day reading a book such as this or learning Masonic Ritual qualifies as such an advancement.

**Dilate – I need not here dilate:** In context, the need for a lengthy explanation is unnecessary.

**Endue:** In context, to provide or endow with the stated ability.

**Enjoin you:** Urge you.

**Entered Apprentice Free Mason:** This term was in use in early Lodges of working Operative Masons (11th-15th century) who built some of Europe's most stunning structures of the times, such as cathedrals. From time-to-time, Lodges took on suitable young boys of good intellect, moral standing and physical fitness to serve as Apprentices. Prospective Apprentices were scrutinised and tested by Members during a Lodge meeting – those approved by the Lodge joined as Apprentices having pledged to abide by a set of rules. The customary training period was seven years and once an Apprentice had shown his initial worth, he was formally 'Entered' into the books of the Guild as an Apprentice, hence Entered Apprentice Free Mason.

**Evince:** Prove or make evident.

**Examination – to undergo an examination when properly called on:** Expressing a willingness to submit to further trials to prove the desired traits and characteristics of a Freemason.

**Exchange the sceptre for the trowel:** Like all Freemasons, when a future monarch joins Freemasonry they start out from the humblest of positions – all Masons being equal. A sceptre, the symbol of regal office, is set aside for the humble trowel. In the early Lodges, the 'humblest of positions' was that of Inner Guard, usually fulfilled by the most recent Initiate who, being armed with trowel, used it to test each Candidate's skin for a sensory response.

**Exhort:** strongly urge/encourage to act.

**Fidelity:** Enduring loyalty.

**Fit and proper person:** Nowadays, someone who has been found to have the desired moral and other essential attributes for admission into Freemasonry. Historically, the above plus being physically fit (lithe) with sound mental faculties and good sensory perception. In medieval times, lefthanded (cack-handed) people were not trusted, so were probably judged to be unfit.

**First or foundation stone:** Also known as a Setting Stone, the Foundation Stone is the most important stone in any masonry construction – its position determines the siting of all the other constituent building blocks. Consequently, it needs to be laid with precision and be perfectly proportioned. All newmade Brethren figuratively lay a foundation stone to signify the beginning of their Masonic journey. The ceremonies for laying physical foundation stones for notable buildings are deeply rooted in history. On occasions, Freemasons have formally participated in such ceremonies; they symbolically confirmed both the precision of the stone and its location.

**Free men:** It is a rule of Freemasonry that no man can become a member if, at the time of Initiation, their liberty is confined, e.g. being imprisoned. In the past this exclusion would also have applied to serfs, bondsmen and slaves.

**Free and Accepted Masons:** Medieval apprenticeships could only be taken up by the children of Freemen who were free to travel. Successfully completing a medieval apprenticeship usually conferred civic freedoms such as being free to work within defined geographical limits; in major cities, apprentices could be enrolled with the city government to become Citizens – the status affording similar working freedoms and privileges. In the early 17th century, men of wealth and position paid to join Lodges as Non-Operative Masons. Some members gained the superior status of 'Accepted Mason'; they were effectively 'accepted' as being equal to Operative members. On the formation of Grand Lodge, Accepted Masons were referred to as being Free & Accepted.

**Free and Accepted or Speculative:** By the mid-17th century the term 'Speculative' was also applied to Non-Operative membership – the use of mathematics in creating schemes for buildings did not require the use of physical tools – such knowledge-based processes were described as being 'speculative'. Ultimately, Free and Accepted or Speculative membership considerably outnumbered Operative Mason membership.

**Gauge: 24 inch Gauge:** A wooden measuring rod or ruler

**Great Architect of the Universe:** A traditional euphemistic reference to the Supreme Being or God.

**Heart – In my heart:** Masonic Ritual stems from a time when people commonly believed that the human brain helped regulate blood temperature (ergo 'hot head', 'letting off steam' etc.) Character, moral judgement etc. were thought to reside in the heart (ergo 'kind-hearted' versus 'cold-hearted')

**Hele:** Is an Old English word which simply means 'to cover up', e.g. enclosing a building by adding a roof to it. May still be in use as a thatching term. Emulation Ritual specifies the correct pronunciation to be 'hail' as in 'nail', but some Lodges pronounce 'heel' instead. The reason given for the latter is that older Masonic Ritual and documents often used memory friendly rhyming phrases ergo the 'heel' pronunciation chimes with the words 'conceal 'and 'reveal' in the same sentence. The planting of bare root trees and shrubs were 'heeled' into the ground to cover up the roots, protecting them from frost. Whichever pronunciation is used, it is correct for that particular Lodge.

**Hoodwink:** Headwear (hood) to close the eyes (wink) possibly Anglo Saxon related to falconry. In Freemasonry, denies the visual perception of the Lodge prior to taking our Obligation; symbolises rebirth rendering us into a state of helplessness whilst accentuating our other senses.

**Indissoluble:** Indestructible.

**Indite:** To record in writing.

**Inviolate: to keep inviolate:** Not to violate or betray.

**Just, perfect and regular:** The open Volume of the Sacred Law makes the Lodge 'just' (correct); no Candidate can be Initiated unless there are a minimum of seven regularly made Masons in attendance, such an minimum attendance makes the Lodge 'perfect' and the display of the Lodge's Warrant (issued by United Grand Lodge) makes it 'regular'.

**Lights in Freemasonry:** The three Great Lights of Freemasonry – the Volume of the Sacred Law [VSL], Square and Compasses – are the primary sources of Masonic enlightenment, guiding the ideal self-regulation of our lives and actions. The VSL is considered the most eminent as it governs our faith. In this particular Masonic context, the word 'Light' simply means 'Knowledge'.

**Meridian:** The sun is at its meridian at noon. The reflection of the full sun in the bottom of a well only happens when the sun was at its meridian.

**North-East corner:** In Speculative Freemasonry, the placing of a foundation stone in the NE Corner is symbolic. The sun rises in the east arcing, through its meridian, to the west where it sets. The ancient world considered the east to be strongly associated with both natural daylight and the enlightenment of education. Conversely, northern Europe was thought of as a place of darkness – shorter solar days and populated by uncivilised, warring tribes. Standing in the NE symbolises leaving the darkness of the non-Masonic world to enter the light of Freemasonry to begin a journey of enlightened discovery. Building from the NE corner optimised the amount of daylight to work in.

**Obtrude:** Become noticeable in an undesirable way.

**Odes:** Masonic hymns and poems – as in our Opening and Closing Odes.

**Operative Masons:** Historically, a qualified Stone Mason who had successfully completed a seven year Apprenticeship. More recently, a qualified person in a recognised construction related profession such as an architect, master builder, civil engineer, surveyor, stone mason etc.

**Ornaments: Masonic Ornaments:** Beautifying objects in tangible form (items adorning a Lodge room) or intangible (desired moral attributes, e.g. Charity).

**Paradox:** An apparently contradictory statement which at first seems absurd, but upon closer examination apparently seems true.

**Peculiar system of morality, veiled in allegory and illustrated by symbols:** Founded on an ethical code (morality) that we can subjectively contemplate and exercise judgement over (veiled in allegory). Freemasonry existed long before most people could read, so symbols served to illustrate the essential Masonic values. In plain English we might simply say, 'A system of self-improvement, gradually revealed in Masonic Ceremonies (stories) working with objects given alternative, morally founded, meanings'.

**Perfect points of my entrance:** Not all Masonic ritual has a ready explanation including this phrase. One academic theory is that the entire Ceremony of Initiation constitutes the 'entrance' into Freemasonry comprising five perfect (principal) points – namely, Preparation (prior to entering the Lodge) Obligation, Sign, Grip or Token and Word. There are other theories, but we return to the point that the original meaning is lost to the mists of time.

**Poniard:** Long bladed, hilted stabbing knife often worn by the upper class, noblemen or knights from the 14th century onwards. Probably originated in France. In some Masonic jurisdictions the Inner Guard is permanently armed with a Poniard, but in some early English Lodges a trowel was used, possibly to avoid bringing an offensive weapon into the Lodge.

**Poor Candidate:** Not physically in possession of any material wealth or valuables including money, metal etc.

**Precepts:** Rules, commands or principles set out to influence actions and thoughts.

**Precludes you from gratifying them:** Prevents you from satisfying them.

**Premise: Premise for your general information…:** State the evidence in support of a conclusion. For example 'Red sky at night, shepherd's delight' – 'Red sky' is the evidence supporting the conclusion that fair weather is in prospect. In context, that '…all Squares, Levels and Perpendiculars' (the evidence) are true and proper Signs to know a Mason by (conclusion).

**Premised: first, as I have already premised:** As I have previously explained.

**Prompt attention to all signs and summonses:** In a modern context, when in receipt of a Lodge Meeting Summons a Brother should promptly inform the Lodge Secretary if he is unable to attend .

**Properly dedicated:** All new Lodges are 'solemnly constituted according to ancient usage' by the Grand Master or his appointed deputy (usually a Provincial Grand Master outside of London). A statement of dedication forms part of the Consecration Ceremony, e.g. dedicated to the service of God etc.

**Prudence, Temperance, Fortitude and Justice:** The four Cardinal Virtues or principal moral virtues, which in today's language equates to Wisdom, Moderation, Courage and Fairness.

**Range under its banners:** Our Lodges be they Grand, Metropolitan, Provincial or individual Craft lodges usually have a bespoke banner, each serving as a proclamation of identity. The Lodge banner is usually displayed in the Lodge room during Regular meetings. On special Masonic and civic occasions (and, where applicable, with the necessary permissions) Freemasons parade, with or without regalia – forming up, or ranging behind the Lodge Banner and its bearer. There is no constitutional requirement for a Lodge to have a banner.

**Rectitude of your actions:** Straightness of your actions; being morally correct.

**Regularity of my initiation:** The Initiation was constitutionally correct being conducted by a Lodge warranted by Grand Lodge. As proof of this, the WM points out to a newly Initiated Brother, the Warrant of the Lodge.

**Regularly assembled***:* A Lodge is 'Regularly Assembled' when it meets on a date and at a place stipulated by its bye-laws, the Lodge warrant is openly on display and a quorum of Brethren is present. For a Degree Ceremony that is a minimum of five Brethren, excluding the Tyler and Candidate, but including two Lodge members – at least one must be an Installed Master.

**Secret arts and hidden mysteries**: The skills and theoretical specialist knowledge of a medieval Operative Freemason which had to be kept secret. Now applied in a modern Speculative setting to the Signs, Tokens and Words of individual Masonic Degrees.

**Sign, Token and Word:** Signs are salutes and other gestures that have an allegorical meaning; Tokens are the grips (handshakes) nowadays solely used in Lodge meetings as a means of identification and the 'Word' was entrusted to us when we were Initiated. All three comprise the Secrets we obligated ourselves to keep as Freemasons.

**Slip shod:** Literally means 'worn down to the heel'. Historically, someone taking a solemn obligation sometimes removed a shoe as an act of submission.

**Solicit:** Asking or seeking to obtain something.

**Square – By acting with him on the square:** Forming a relationship founded on sound moral principles.

**State of Darkness:** Unable to perceive light due to being 'hoodwinked'.

**Stately and superb edifices:** Buildings of imposing scale and appearance.

**Superfluous knobs and excrescences:** Unattractive, unwanted features present on an unworked stone.

**Superstructure:** This is the visible part of a construction that rises from the base line of its 'hidden from view' foundations.

**Time immemorial**: A distant time without any surviving records or memories.

**VSL:** Volume of the Sacred Law.

**Warranted Lodge:** Under the English Constitution, a Lodge chartered by Warrant by the United Grand Lodge of England and accordingly observes UGLE's *Book of Constitutions*.

**Without equivocation:** Without uncertainty or doubt.


## Explanations *of* other common Masonic Terms

**Chair or Throne of King Solomon:** The chair from which the Worshipful Master rules the Lodge.

**FMT:** Formerly *Freemasonry Today*, now just *FMT*, the quarterly Freemasons' magazine published under the auspices of UGLE.

**Grand Lodge Above:** When a Brother expires, he is said to have 'passed to the Grand Lodge above'. A euphemism for the afterlife. It is customary for an obituary to be presented at the beginning of the next Lodge Meeting, at the conclusion of which Brethren stand, 'in respect of departed merit'.

**Local Workings:** The majority of Lodges working with Emulation Ritual have some deviations from the pure Emulation Ritual. These sometimes occur for historical reasons or have resulted from longstanding uncorrected errors becoming ingrained when Ritual was orally passed down. Such differences make visiting other Lodges really interesting – no two Lodges are the same, although the underlying Masonic philosophy remains constant.

**LoI:** The abbreviation for a 'Lodge of Instruction'. In the early days of Freemasonry, Ritual was learnt in the oral tradition. Brethren attended Lodges of Instruction primarily to memorise and learn more about Masonic Ritual. The older, more experienced Brethren passed on their knowledge to the succeeding generation who could then practice reciting their Masonic Ritual in a friendly, informal setting.

**LoR:** The abbreviation for a Lodge of Rehearsal, where a Master and his team of Officers rehearse impending Ceremonies. If a Ceremony of Initiation is being rehearsed by your Lodge, consider volunteering as the Candidate to gain a deeper understanding of the Ceremony.

**Masonic Fire:** Not all Lodges employ Masonic Fire as part of their Festive Board routine. The Fire usually involves the striking of a miniature gavel or firing glass (a special toasting glass with a thick glass orb reinforcing the base) on the dining table which can be followed up with hand gestures with, or without, singing. Clapping is sometimes used in lieu of banging the table. There can also be sequential firing by the Brethren following the toast to a new Initiate. The practice varies from Lodge to Lodge, so take care when visiting a Lodge for the first time. Firing possibly dates back to the 17th century when toasts at major civic events were often celebrated by flintlock pistol fire. Charging your glass (pistol); raising and draining the contents followed by banging the glass onto the table, replicating the sound of gunfire. Clearly there were problems discharging firearms indoors, so suitable sound effects were contrived.

**MCF:** The Masonic Charitable Foundation.

**M-Form /P-Form :** This is the form we signed to apply to become a Freemason – it is also used to become a Joining Member of another Lodge, or to re-join a Lodge in which membership was previously held. The M-Form is used by Metropolitan Grand Lodge; the P-Form is the Provincial Grand Lodge equivalent.

**On the Square:** Someone is said to be 'on the Square' if they are a member of a Craft Lodge – a Freemason.

**Preceptor:** The title given to the Brother running the Lodge of Instruction, often the Bro Director of Ceremonies.

**Squaring the Lodge:** In the early days of Speculative Freemasonry, Lodges typically met in a private room within a public house or coffee house. The Tyler, who was responsible for setting up the Lodge, would have chalked or charcoaled the lodge layout onto the floorboards, sweeping the markings away at the meeting's end, so no trace was left behind for non-Masonic eyes to see. So as not to smudge or erase the Tyler's work during the meeting, Brethren would carefully square the Lodge making soldier like, precision 90 degree turns. Squaring in this way has no actual military connection.

**UGLE:** The accepted abbreviation for the United Grand Lodge of England.

# Part 6

# Mastering Masonic Ritual

*the* 5 *Minute* Ritualist

# Mastering Masonic Ritual - *Introduction*

Do you find the prospect or experience of memorising Masonic Ritual challenging or even daunting? The purpose of this section is to demonstrate a simple, scientifically founded method for memorising Masonic Ritual called *The 5-Minute Ritualist* (5-MR). The associated 5-MR Stationery is available to download as MS Word documents from *The New Mason's Friend* page on the *Lewis Masonic* website. 5-MR can be used to memorise any text be it Masonic Ritual, poetry, lines for a play, proposal for a pay rise – anything you like.

The 5-MR system is easy to work with and can be up and running in a few minutes. What is more, once primed with our target Ritual, the stationery can be electronically transferred (e.g. as a pdf file) to a personal mobile 'phone or tablet for short, private memorisation sessions on the move. Apple devotees should be able to convert the MS Word files. Saving the 5-MR files as document templates means they will always be to hand as stationery items.

For those of us never having learnt anything by rote before – good news – what follows is a 'quick start' induction with three demonstration workings:

1. **Opening Ode**

2. **Closing Ode**

3. **Questions & Answers leading to the Second Degree**
   (Ceremony of Passing – Fellow Craft)

**Note:** *If you have already memorised all of these elements, use the 5-MR stationery to memorise another Ritual working - perhaps the Working Tools of an EAFM. Talk to your Mentor, Brother Director of Ceremonies, or Lodge of Instruction Preceptor to help choose a suitable Ritual working.*

Before we make a start, let us very briefly consider why we commit Masonic Ritual to memory.

# Why We Memorise Masonic Ritual

Firstly, the memorisation effort allows us to reflect upon and think more deeply about the underlying Masonic teachings – these gain greater resonance than would otherwise be the case. A long-term memory of the Working Tools of an EAFM means these can be readily called to mind with all their associated symbolic meanings.

A second point is that as Ritualists we are making a positive contribution to the overall wellbeing of our Lodge. Memorised Ritual can be likened to a store of energy with our Lodge serving as a Ritual battery. The better the overall Ritual charge the greater qualitative potential our Lodge has to conduct accomplished Ceremonies. A well charged Lodge Ritual battery will help maximise both visitors and new member recruitment numbers – success tends to breed even more success.

The third point is of a qualitative nature. Well memorised Ritual can be called to mind and recited almost effortlessly, which means we have a greater capacity to focus on presentation qualities. Factors such as intonation, adjustments to pitch and pace etc. This enables our words to be genuinely expressed with sincerity and conviction.

For those of us who find speaking before an audience a rather daunting prospect there is a glowing opportunity to boost our confidence. We are always among friends in the Lodge who will support us in making that great Masonic journey from student to teacher. Freemasonry's self-improvement aims certainly embrace the gaining of confidence and competence in the field of human communications. Presenting Ritual in Lodge – just talking to friends!

Finally, a human brain needs to engage in a broad range of tasks to remain healthy; memorising Masonic Ritual in 5-20 minute sessions makes a positive contribution in this regard. Many Brethren find the experience gives them a lift – rather like a mini Masonic meeting; they also feel that the art of memorisation becomes easier with regular practice.

*Time to explore our Memory!*

# The Formation of Long-Term Memory

Psychologists describe human memory formation in three stages, namely:

- **Sensory Memory**
  *sight, hearing, taste, touch, smell, pain + emotional feelings*

- **Working Memory**
  *formerly called Short-Term Memory*

- **Long-Term Memory**

**Sensory Memory:** Our senses convey our experience of external events to our Sensory Memory. The fate of sensory data is that it is either ignored by our brains because it is of no interest, or it is 'perceived'. Whilst sensory memory data is generally short-lived, only the 'perceived 'data can endure long enough to transit to our Working Memory.

**Working Memory:** Can hold 4-7 bits of sensory data, such as a small number of known words, for up to 30 seconds. Through a process called Encoding, some information transits from our Working Memory for archive processing to Long-Term Memory, stored as Pictures (words comprise a series of 'letter' pictures), Sounds and Facts/Meanings. Within Working Memory, we can make a conscious decision to encode facts, such as learning Masonic Ritual, to Long-Term Memory, forming what psychologists call Explicit Memory. By way of contrast, Implicit Memory describes the storage of information we do not actively concentrate on, e.g. yesterday's weather. This could include words and procedural structures of Lodge meetings our brains have unconsciously registered from our regular attendance. We just seem to instinctively know what is coming next.

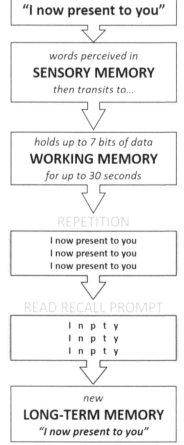

Our Working Memory can also retrieve information from our Long-Term Memory. In this way, a sound might remind us of a special event we experienced a long time ago. It also functions like a two-way valve – we can either encode new information to Long-Term Memory (learning) or we can retrieve existing memories for further processing (thinking) – we cannot do both simultaneously.

**Chunking:** This is the term applied to breaking down written information into smaller, Working Memory friendly portions (4-7 words). This helps to regulate the streaming process of Encoding to Long-Term Memory by not overloading our Working Memory. When we 'chunk' Ritual to memorise, we need to make sure each chunk includes complete phrases. Poets, lyricists, advertising copywriters etc. all use 'chunking' strategies to make their words easier to remember, as will rhymes and rhythmic syncopation (beat).

**Comprehension:** Memorising how a word sounds requires only shallow processing, i.e. encoding just as a sound without understanding its meaning. Encoding words contextually (semantically) requires much deeper processing. Trying to learn Masonic Ritual without a basic comprehension of all the archaic language makes our challenge unnecessarily harder and frustrating. Once we comprehend all the words in their proper context, we will be able to restate the Ritual using everyday language; this creates the contextual foundations upon which we can build a long-term memory of our target Ritual.

**Note:** The New Mason's Friend *has a handy glossary explaining the archaic content of the Ceremony of Initiation and the Q & A leading to the Second Degree.*

**Recall Fading:** Between Ritual encoding sessions, our initial Shallow Processed memory of the words begins to fade. We need to routinely test and refresh our memory in the early days of learning something new. The longer the interval between learning sessions, the greater the amount of memory recall fading we will need to restore. Consequently, 5-MR works best on a little but often basis, e.g. 5-20 minutes per encoding session. In effect, the initial learning process tends to be of a two steps forward, one step back nature and we need to be mentally prepared for this to happen. Frequent repetition ultimately creates a fade resistant, Deep Processed, long-term memory of the work. Our memorised words will seem to trip effortlessly off our tongues.

# Introducing the 5-Minute Ritualist (5-MR) Memory System

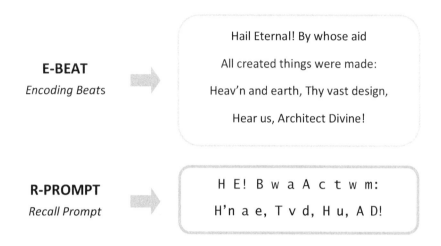

**E-BEAT**
*Encoding Beats*

Hail Eternal! By whose aid

All created things were made:

Heav'n and earth, Thy vast design,

Hear us, Architect Divine!

**R-PROMPT**
*Recall Prompt*

H E! B w a A c t w m:

H'n a e, T v d, H u, A D!

**Encoding-Beats:** Many professional actors learn their lines by splitting them into memory friendly chunks called Beats. These are then Encoded to Long Term Memory through repetition. The ideal 5-MR layout centres the text into a list format to avoid concentration breaking lateral eye movement. Hunters' eyes are not designed to look sideways – hunters move their heads sideways to keep their central visual sweet spot locked onto lunch! Avoiding lateral eye movement = high concentration. To avoid overloading our Working Memory any single line of chunked text should have no more than seven words.

**Recall Prompt:** 5-MR goes even further by editing our target Ritual into a Recall Prompt. This consists of the first letter of each word (upper and lower case observed) and all punctuation marks including apostrophes and any numerals. This helps us to 'see' the words in the mind's eye which helps to accelerate the encoding process.

The following workings have been fully 5-MR processed and are ready to memorise straight from the page:

1. **Opening Ode**

2. **Closing Ode**

3. **Questions & Answers leading to the Second Degree** (Fellow Craft)

# The Opening Ode

Hail Eternal! By whose aid

All created things were made:

Heav'n and earth, Thy vast design,

Hear us, Architect Divine!

**5-MR Methodology – Part 1**: Read or recite the first two lines of the first E-Beat 4-6 times and then drop your eyes to the R-Prompt and try to recite the words.

H E! B w a A c t w m:

H'n a e, T v d, H u, A D!

Repeat this cycle until the first two lines can be accurately and confidently recited from the R-Prompt, then repeat the process for the second two lines.

May our work, begun in Thee,

Ever blessed with order be,

And may we, when labours cease,

Part in harmony and peace.

Once able to recite the whole verse from the R-Prompt the time has arrived to see if we can recite the whole verse from memory without any prompts.

M o w, b i T, E b w o b,

A m w, w l c, p i h a p.

This discloses any words or phrases that have not quite made it into our Long-Term Memory – we simply return to the R-Prompt for a little more repetition until we can comfortably and confidently recite the words from memory.

By Thy glorious Majesty

By the trust we place in Thee

By the badge and mystic sign

Hear us, Architect Divine!

**Repeat Part 1 for each verse.**

B T g M – B t t w p i T

B t b a m s – H u, A D!

# The Opening Ode

## R-CARD
*Recall Card*

H E! B w a A c t w m:

H'n a e, T v d, H u, A D!


M o w, b i T, E b w o b,

A m w, w l c, p i h a p.


B T g M – B t t w p i T

B t b a m s – H u, A D!

**5-MR Methodology – Part 2**:
Once the three individual verses have been memorised, we are ready to connect the three verses by trying to read or recite them from the R-Card opposite:

We can go back to the E-Beats to repair any memory lapses. Once we can comfortably recite the three verses from the R-Card, we can take the third step.

**5-MR Methodology – Part 3**:
Now we can try an unprompted recital, cycling back to the R-Card or E-Beats to repair any memory lapses until we can confidently and correctly recite all the words without any prompting.

**5-MR Methodology – Part 4**: To mitigate memory fading, recite the work 1-3 times each day. When our recall feels both spontaneous and effortless, we can celebrate the attainment of Deep Processed Long-Term Memory formation. Just rehearse 1-2 times a month to keep it alive – simply singing the words at Lodge Meetings should suffice.

# The Closing Ode

Now the evening shadows closing,

Warn from toil to peaceful rest,

Mystic arts and rites reposing,

Sacred in each faithful breast.

---

N t e s c, W f t t p r,

M a a r r, S i e f b.

---

God of Light! Whose love unceasing,

Doth to all Thy works extend,

Crown our Order with Thy blessing,

Build; sustain us to the end.

---

G of L! W l u, D t a T w e,

C o O w T b, B; s u t t e.

---

Humbly now we bow before Thee

Grateful for Thy aid Divine:

Everlasting power and glory,

Mighty Architect! be Thine.

---

H n w b b T G f T a D;

E p a g, M A! b T.

**Deep Processing – Recall Maintenance:** 5-MR helps us to achieve Deep Processing status, so we can build and maintain an 'always on call' repertoire of Masonic Ritual. The amount of rehearsal repetition required to arrive at the destination of effortless recall will vary from Brother to Brother – it is certainly attainable without becoming obsessive. Once achieved, all that is required is an occasional dusting off – rehearsing once or twice a month. We should run regular maintenance recitations of our Ritual repertoire. Minor errors have a habit of sneaking in – human memory is a fickle thing.

## R - CARD

*Recall Card*

N t e s c, W f t t p r,

M a a r r, S i e f b.

G of L! W l u, D t a T w e,

C o O w T b, B; s u t t e.

H n w b b T G f T a D;

E p a g, M A! b T.

# Q's and A's leading to the Ceremony of Passing

Medieval Apprentices would have had their knowledge routinely examined, including verbally answering a series of questions – Speculative Freemasonry emulates this.

Accordingly, as EAFM's, we are invited to learn and recite the responses to a set of 11 questions before being Passed to the Second Degree. For many of us, this may well be our first attempt at learning something by rote in adulthood. This proposes a 12th question – do we really understand the questions and their responses? If the answer is 'no', then do we really have enough Masonic knowledge to be taking the next step?

Nowadays, Freemasonry recognises such issues and in addition to mentoring services there are a number of explanatory support publications including this book. However, the New Mason's Friend goes an extra mile by systematically setting everything up ready to memorise straight from the page. This is the best approach to comprehending and memorising the responses:

- Start by reading through all the questions and answers a couple of times to become familiar with them.

- Read through them again, this time reading the explanation of each question to clarify the archaic language content.

- Once the above are completed, we can start to memorise our answers using the 4-Part methodology employed for memorising the Opening & Closing Odes.

Happily, some of the answers are very short.

**Tip:** *There is a single Recall-Card for encoding the answers for all 11 questions – consider scanning or photocopying this – tuck a paper copy into a wallet or electronically transfer to a mobile device. Got a spare minute or two? Test yourself!*

*Do not worry if you lose the R-Card – it is absolutely meaningless to anyone other than Freemason.*

*It is a practical anytime, anyplace, anywhere working tool.*

# Q. 1 Where were you first prepared to be made a Mason?

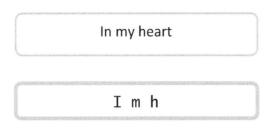

In my heart

I m h

**Explanation:** Masonic Ritual stems from a time when people commonly believed that the sole purpose of the human brain was to help regulate blood temperature (ergo, hot head; letting off steam etc.) Character, moral judgement etc. were thought to emanate from the heart (ergo, kind-hearted versus cold-hearted) Remember when we considered the rationale for our sensory deprivation whilst preparing for our Ceremony of Initiation? One of the reasons given in the Emulation Masonic Lectures was, 'that our hearts should conceive before our eyes perceive'. We felt a strong emotional or spiritual connection to Freemasonry well before our Initiation.

# Q. 2 Where next?

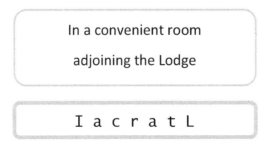

In a convenient room

adjoining the Lodge

I a c r a t L

**Explanation:** None required.

## Q. 3 Describe the mode of your preparation

I was **d...v...d** of **m....l**

and **h...w...d.**

My **r a, l b** and **k**

were made **b**

my **r h** was **s s**

and a **c t**

placed about my **n**

I w d o m a h.

M r a, l b a k w m b

m r h w s s

a a c t p a m n

**Explanation:** This summarises how the Tyler prepared us for Initiation – some of the abbreviated words are dealt with in the First Degree glossary, others are body parts.

**Note:** *To preserve Masonic exclusivity, some words are partially omitted'. Seek advice from an experienced Brother if you do not know/remember any of these words. This helps to keep our Ritual exclusively within a Masonic universe – in earlier times, our forebears generally learnt their Ritual by listening to other Brethren reciting it aloud.*

## Q. 4 Where were you made a Mason?

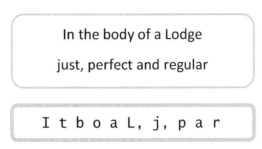

In the body of a Lodge

just, perfect and regular

I t b o a L, j, p a r

**Explanation: just, perfect and regular:** The open Volume of the Sacred Law makes the Lodge 'just' (correct); no Candidate can be Initiated unless there are a minimum of seven regularly made Masons in attendance, such minimum attendance makes the Lodge 'perfect' and the display of the Lodge's Warrant (issued by United Grand Lodge) makes it 'regular'.

**Memorisation Tip:** *'just, perfect, regular' run in first letter alphabetical order..*

## Q. 5 And when?

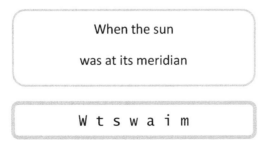

When the sun

was at its meridian

W t s w a i m

**Explanation:** The sun is at its meridian at noon.

## Q. 6 In this country Freemasons' Lodges are usually held in the evening; how do you account for that which at first view appears a paradox?

The earth

constantly revolving

on its axis

in its orbit round the sun

and Freemasonry

being universally

spread over its surface,

it necessarily follows

that the sun

must always be

at its meridian

with respect to Freemasonry

```
T  e  c  r  o  i  a  i  i  o  r  t  s
   a  F  b  u  s  o  i  s  ,  i  n  f
t  t  s  m  a  b  a  i  m  w  r  t  F
```

**Explanation: Freemasonry being universally spread over its surface:** Freemasons' Lodges can be found all around the world – Asia, the Americas, Europe, Africa, the Antipodes and the Far East – the sun literally never sets on Freemasonry! **Paradox:** An apparently contradictory statement which at first seems absurd, but upon closer examination apparently seems true.

# Q. 7 What is Freemasonry?

A peculiar system of morality,

veiled in allegory

and illustrated by symbols

A p s o m,

v i a a i b s

**Explanation:** 'A peculiar system of morality': A unique system of self-improvement. 'veiled in allegory': gradually revealed by Masonic Ceremony themes (allegorical stories) 'and illustrated by symbols': and illustrated by objects given morally founded, alternative meanings.

# Q. 8 Name the grand principles on which the Order is founded

Brotherly love,

relief and truth

B l, r a t

**Explanation:** In the modern idiom 'True friendship, supporting those in need and personal integrity'.

## Q. 9 Who are fit and proper persons to be made Masons?

Just, upright and free men,

of mature age,

sound judgment,

and strict morals

J, u a f m,

o m a, s j, a s m

**Explanation: Free men:** It is a rule of Freemasonry that no one can become a member if, at the time of Initiation, their liberty is confined, e.g. being imprisoned. In the past this exclusion also applied to those in bondage and in the medieval Operative past, would also have included the peasant classes with the exception of 'Freemen'. It is considered that the originators of Speculative Freemasonry subscribed to the Pythagorean wisdom that physical liberty and the freedom to think were inextricably linked. Those so constrained were not in control of their destinies, so could not derive any benefits from Freemasonry until their circumstances changed.

**Mature Age:** Presently, no one under the age of 21 years can be made a Mason, the only exception are Candidates of Masonic parentage (a Lewis) when the minimum age is 18 years.

# Q. 10  How do you know yourself to be a Mason?

By the regularity

of my initiation,

repeated trials

and approbations,

and a willingness

at all times

to undergo an examination

when properly called on

B t r o m I,

r t a a,

a a w a a t

t u a e w p c o

**Explanation:** 'By the regularity of my Initiation': Your Initiation was constitutionally correct being conducted by a Lodge warranted by Grand Lodge. As proof of this, the WM points out to all newly Initiated Brethren, the Warrant of the Lodge.

'Repeated trials and approbations': Repeated tests and approvals.

'To undergo an examination when properly called on': Expressing a willingness to submit to further trials to prove the desired traits, knowledge and characteristics of a Freemason.

## Q. 11 How do you demonstrate the proof of your being a Mason to others?

> By signs, tokens,
>
> and the perfect points
>
> of my entrance

> B s, t, a t p p o m e

**Explanation: Signs, tokens:** Signs are salutes and other hand gestures that have an allegorical meaning; Tokens are the grips (handshakes) nowadays solely used in Lodge as a means of identification.

**Perfect Points of my entrance:** Not all Masonic ritual has a ready explanation including this phrase. One academic theory is that the entire Ceremony of Initiation constitutes the 'entrance' into Freemasonry comprising five perfect (principal) points – namely:

1.   **Preparation** (prior to entering the Lodge)

2.   **Obligation**

3.   **Sign**

4.   **Grip** or **Token**

5.   **Word**

There are other theories, but we return to the point that the original meaning is lost to the mists of time.

# Questions & Answers Recall Card

The R-Card below summarises in list form the questions and their R-Prompt responses. This can be copied and safely used when we are on the move (as can any R-Card) given it will not make any sense to anyone who is not a Freemason. It is simply an 'any time, any place, anywhere' Masonic Ritual memorisation tool. If we get stuck on a word whilst out and about, we can always 'phone a Masonic friend to seek relief!

Where first prepared

I m h

Where next

I a c r a t L

Mode of preparation

I w d o m a h.
M r a, l b a k w m b
m r h w s s
a a c t p a m n

Where made a M

I t b o a L, j, p a r

When

W t s w a i m

Appears a paradox

T e c r o i a
i i o r t s
a F b u s o i s,
i n f
t t s m a b a i m
w r t F

What is F

A p s o m
v i a a i b s

Name grand principles

B l, r a t

Who are fit and proper

J, u a f m,
o m a, s j, a s m

Know yourself to be a M

B t r o m I, r t a a,
a a w a a t
t u a e w p c o

Demonstrate the proof

B s, t, a t p p o m e

# Question List

**Ready for an unprompted test?**

Use the **Question List** prompt below to give it a go:

Where first prepared

Where next

Mode of preparation

Where made a M

And when

First view appears a paradox

What is Freemasonry

Name the grand principles

Who are fit and proper persons

How do you know yourself to be a M

How do you demonstrate the proof

**Tips:**

**1.** Once you can confidently recite the answers without prompting continue to rehearse them if you wish to achieve effortless Deep Process recall status.

**2.** Occasionally check the accuracy of your recall against the E-Beats – substitute words sometimes sneak in without our noticing.

# Managing Ritual Presentation Expectations

Humankind got to where it is today by people making mistakes and learning how to avoid them in the future. The same principle absolutely applies to presenting Masonic Ritual – every experienced Ritualist will never forget their own steep learning curve. Brethren admire, support and empathise with any Brother who is prepared to try presenting Masonic Ritual. The following may also help:

- If our Lodge is blessed with one or more accomplished Ritualists, we can try asking for some advice, tips etc. – we might even end up with the blessing of being mentored.

- By rehearsing our Ritual in front of a mirror (ideally full length) we can work on improving any areas of concern – seeing is believing. This also helps us to monitor our posture, hand gestures, salutes etc.

- Before our presentation (actual and rehearsal) we could ask our Bro Director of Ceremonies to give us an honest post-presentation appraisal to help us improve – *this says we are open to constructive, improvement pointers. It also signals that we are committed to presenting Ritual in the future and actively seeking to improve.*

- Similarly or alternatively, seek a constructive review from any close Masonic friends.

## Managing Confidence and Competences

It is perfectly natural to have some pre-presentation negative thoughts but holding onto them, so they take root and grow, helps no one. We need positive counterpoints to keep any negative vibes in the distant background where they will help motivate us to do the work.

The three most common 'negatives' for presenting Masonic Ritual are:

- Forgetting our words – *losing our place*

- Freezing midst presentation

- Poor performance perception

Every Ritualist, irrespective of experience, will occasionally stumble over their words – it is simply a common occupational hazard. For example, an unexpected sound might cause us to lose concentration. The skill lies in the requesting and provision of a prompt. We need to find out who will be prompting us during the meeting – typically it falls to the Bro Director of Ceremonies or the ADC. Agreeing in advance how prompting will work in practice will help allay concerns over any negative impact. Consider the following simple protocol:

- We need to agree a discreet prompt request signal with our Prompter. For example, we might simply agree to make direct eye contact with our Prompter – no direct eye contact – no prompt required.

- Due to the nature of Chaining, the prompt should never be a single word, but four or more words, one or two complete phrases. Picking up a chain sequence is like threading cotton through the eye of a needle – we need a short run of cotton, not the meanest of pinches, to pick up the thread again.

- There is no need for us to articulate a request for a prompt or apologise for faltering – we just need to make a quick, seamless, 'business as usual' recovery.

# Managing our Nerves

When presenting Masonic Ritual in front of a live audience (including formal rehearsals) our Amygdala's intervention (an old, evolutionary part of the human brain located just above the brain stem) triggers the release of adrenalin into our blood stream – consequently, we may experience some of the following reactions:

- Sweaty palms
- Loss of voice control – *sounds shaky*
- Accelerated heartbeat
- Shortness of breath – *weighted feeling*
- Butterflies or distressed stomach

These are the symptoms of 'performance anxiety', which can usually be surmounted or minimised, by duping the Amygdala into believing the threat has passed, so turning off the adrenalin tap.

**Here are three effective Amygdala taming actions:**

1. **Breathing Exercise:** Breathe out to a slow count of four, breathe in normally – this will help to regulate our breathing. Not only can we do this exercise just before our presentation starts, but also during it when reaching a natural pause point. Breathing out more slowly tells our Amygdala that we are relaxed, the threat has passed, and no more adrenalin is required, thank you very much!

   **Tip:** *Run through the Ritual using the Recall Card and mark up all the natural pause points where we can use this breathing technique, e.g. when pointing out objects – usually, there are more opportunities than we might think.*

2. **Slow the Presentation Down:** Slowing down our delivery a notch has a calming effect, stemming the flow of adrenalin into our circulatory system, thus helping to regulate our breathing. By slowing down, we are again telling our Amygdala that the 'threat' has passed. In any event, our presentation should be of a measured pace, so the Candidate can absorb what is being communicated.

3.  **Endorphin Release:** Our bodies release endorphins when reacting to certain conditions. These powerful chemicals interact with receptor cells making us feel positive and happy. Endorphin release is triggered naturally when we genuinely smile and socially engage with friends, so we should greet every Brother attending the meeting and naturally smile our way round the Lodge room.

Planning and preparing to experience some form of performance anxiety will, in itself, help us to both minimise and manage any symptoms. The singularly most important thing to remember is:

*In our Lodge Meetings*

*we are always truly among friends.*

*Hold onto such positive thoughts –*

*they have a great reassuring influence –*

*we are continuously supported!*

## Final Words...

This brings us to the end of *The New Mason's Friend*, and hopefully you are now set fair for your continuing journey as a Freemason.

May that be a long, highly rewarding and pleasurable experience.

Whilst sorry to part, we will happily meet again each time you return to the pages of *The New Mason's Friend*, and perhaps *The 5-Minute Ritualist* as well.

*Kim March* PM

## Final Symbol...

(Mystified? - See page 13)

SD - #0080 - 240521 - C0 - 210/148/9 - PB - 9780853185741